STILL
FLYING

STILL
FLYING

E. L. CORNWELL

LONDON

IAN ALLAN LTD

First published 1979

ISBN 0 7110 0905 8

Published by Ian Allan Ltd, Shepperton, Surrey;
and printed in the United Kingdom by
Ian Allan Printing Ltd

Below: Perfectly caught on a circuit of Old Warden,
one of Shuttleworth Trust's two Gloster Gladiators
(the other is on loan to the FAA Museum).
Air Portraits

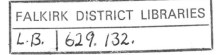

Contents

Battle of Britain Memorial Flight

Sqn Ldr K. R. Jackson AFC

THE BATTLE OF BRITAIN Memorial Flight maintains in fully flying condition some of the most famous Royal Air Force aircraft of World War II. To the many hundreds of thousands who yearly are able to see the gracefulness of these aircraft in flight and hear the rhythm of their Rolls-Royce Merlin and Griffon engines (surely the most beautiful sound in the world for aviation enthusiasts) they epitomise the spirit and traditions of the Royal Air Force and Allied Air Forces forged in the turmoil of war.

The tasks of the BBMF today are to preserve and present the living history of the RAF's most memorable era in its 60-year history. In the following paragraphs it is hoped to give the reader an insight into the relatively short history of the Flight; the selection and training of the aircrew who are privileged to fly these revered and irreplaceable aircraft; the problems of keeping historic aircraft in flying condition and the efforts made by the small, but dedicated, team of technicians on the Flight and the support given them by the engineering organisation of the RAF, the British aviation industry and individual aviation enthusiasts nationwide. Finally, the problems of planning and executing up to 120 displays in an average season will be discussed with the particular problems of a typical display weekend as seen by the air and ground crews.

The Battle of Britain Memorial Flight was formed at Biggin Hill on 11 July 1957, but, due to a rapid cutback in the number of operational RAF airfields around that time, the Flight was to move in quick succession to North Weald and Martlesham Heath in 1958, to Horsham St Faith in 1960 and to Coltishall in 1964. The Flight was destined to remain at that historic 1940 fighter base for a full 12 years until 1 March 1976, when it was moved to its present location at Royal Air Force Coningsby in Lincolnshire. This last move was found necessary due to the rapid build-up of the Jaguar force at Coltishall which put an unacceptable strain on the facilities available at that station.

The types and numbers of aircraft have fluctuated over the years but the current complement consists of two Griffon-powered Spitfires, two Merlin-powered Spitfires, two Hurricanes and one Lancaster. Most of the aircraft had historically interesting backgrounds before joining the Flight. The Royal Air Force Board decided in 1977 to change each aircraft's lettering at every major servicing, which is carried out every four years at RAF Kemble in Gloucestershire, to a different squadron number. The first two aircraft to appear in 'new' squadron markings will be Spitfire Mk IIa P7350, which will change from ZH-T (266 Sqn) to QV-B (19 Sqn), and Hurricane Mk IIc PZ865 which will change from DT-A (257 Sqn) to JU-Q (111 Sqn). The decision to rotate squadron markings was made so that as many as possible of the famous squadrons which fought in the Battle of Britain and the bomber offensive over Europe can be represented by an historic aircraft of the BBMF for a four-year period.

All aircrew who fly BBMF aircraft take on the commitment as a secondary duty, that is to say it is not a full-time occupation but is fitted in around their primary task. It is often difficult to convince some spectators at weekend air displays that that is the case and that all aircrew will be expected to be back at their normal place of duty first thing on the following Monday morning.

One question that is often asked is 'how do pilots manage to get selected to fly BBMF aircraft?' To start with, they are all volunteers, not that there has ever been any shortage of those for such a privilege. They are only approved to fly with the BBMF after a carefully controlled sequence of training which will be described later. Because of the type and amount of previous flying experience required all aircrew will almost certainly be over the age of 30. It is also highly likely that they will be on ground tours such as simulator instructing, air traffic controlling or operations. The reason for this is that they are in a better position to arrange their work-load or shifts to

Above: Battle of Britain Memorial Flight transit formation, consisting of Lancaster B1 PA474 *City of Lincoln*, Hurricane IIc PZ865 DT-A and Spitfire XIX PM631 AD-C, as seen by thousands throughout the display flying season. / *Air Portraits*

meet the requirements of the Flight. For the very same reason, the few aircrew who are in flying appointments will probably be employed as staff pilots or instructors and it is only rarely that front-line squadron pilots, who are prone to long detachments away from base during exercises, plus a fair number of weekend working days, are considered due to the fact that they might not be available when required. One final point that narrows down the selection field considerably is that, for preference, aircrews should be based at the 'home' of the BBMF — RAF Coningsby — or at least within easy travelling distance.

Of the five or six pilots who fly the Spitfires and Hurricanes in any one season, two are chosen due to their appointment. One, of course, is always the Station Commander who must be fully au fait with the limitations and capabilities of all aircraft on his station. He must also have a deep insight into the problems of display flying that crews under his command are likely to meet. The second semi-permanent pilot, due to appointment, will almost invariably be the Officer Commanding the Operations Wing who, in effect, is the senior air executive responsible to the Station Commander for all flying and related matters on his station. The problem of providing aircrew for the manning of the Lancaster was, until recently, far less troublesome. By arrangement between 11 Group (Fighters) which controls the BBMF, and 1 Group (Bombers), the latter undertook to provide complete Lancaster crews as and when required. The crew was always formed from members of the Hastings Flight of 230 OCU at RAF Scampton. However, the very last Hastings flight was made in August 1977 and in future years it is planned to man the Lancaster with pilots, navigators and flight engineers who have had recent experience on the Shackleton aircraft after the last of the Hastings/Lancaster-trained aircrew retire.

On average, two new Spitfire/Hurricane pilots are required at the start of each season and, starting in November, a fly-off is held among the volunteers to try and decide which two are most likely to become not only good display pilots but, of greater importance, safe operators of BBMF's historic and irreplaceable aircraft. If the contest, which is flown on a Chipmunk, should be declared a dead heat for one of the vacancies, previous experience will obviously have to count in the final selection. For the lucky two the training will follow a standard pattern which is worth looking at in a little detail. Due to the fact that very few dual-control Spitfires were ever built, most Spitfire pilots have, over the years from 1936 onwards, made their first-ever flight on type solo. The same applies to this day but, to be fair, it is safe to say that a far more thorough grounding is given before a first Spitfire solo flight on the BBMF than was ever possible in the past. To start with, a selected pilot will be given up to 25 hours on the Chipmunk aircraft. This will not only re-educate him on piston-engined aircraft techniques, but will also give him invaluable experience in the control of 'swing' in cross-winds, which is a feature of all tail-wheel aircraft as opposed to the modern nose-wheel types where swing tends to be self-correcting.

Towards the end of the 25 hours most of the flying will be carried out from the back seat of the Chipmunk which increases the amount of nose in front of the pilot and reduces the amount of forward vision. In fact, flying the Chipmunk from the rear seat is very similar to flying the small (Merlin-powered) Spitfires as far as what can be seen ahead during landing and take-off is concerned. Having successfully completed the Chipmunk phase to the satisfaction of the BBMF Training Officer, who is usually the senior Spitfire pilot of the

7

Flight, the budding Spitfire pilot will be detached to the A&AAE at Boscombe Down for a short course on one of the three remaining Harvard aircraft still in RAF colours. The Harvard has always been well known, perhaps even notorious, for its hefty swing during landings, even in very moderate cross-winds. It has often been said that if you can master the Harvard you have very little to fear from other single-engined aircraft. Be that as it may, the very first flight in a historic aircraft on return to Coningsby will be in one of the two Hurricanes and not a Spitfire. The Hurricane sits higher off the ground than a Spitfire and, of even more importance, the main undercarriage wheels are set further apart, making the Hurricane far less likely to swing, and easier to correct if it should. After two or three hours on the Hurricane the big day arrives for the first solo on the Spitfire, the most famous British fighter of all time, although it is worth noting that Hurricanes shot down more enemy aircraft than any other type during the Battle of Britain. The first solo will be flown on one of the Merlin-powered Spitfires as the engine develops far less power than the Griffon and there is therefore less potential swing, especially during take-offs.

The reader will no doubt have gathered by now that the biggest problem in operating single-engined tail-wheeled aircraft is swing on take-off and landing. In nil wind conditions the swing will be predictable; always in the opposite direction to the rotation of the

Above: PA474 pictured by Dennis Calvert in May 1977 during a photographic session to commemorate the 617 Sqn Dams raid. Low-level runs were made over the Derwent Water dam. / *Inter-Air Press*

Above right: Hurricane IIc PZ865, last Hurricane built, carrying 257 (Burma) Sqn letters DT and Wg Cdr Standford Tuck's personal aircraft letter A — and its borrowed four-bladed propeller. / *Austin J. Brown*

Right: PZ865 again, pictured at the French Air Show at Le Bourget in June 1977 under the nose of Euroworld's B17G N17TE from Duxford. / *Inter-Air Press*

propeller. However, in any cross-wind the swing will be either accentuated, reduced, cancelled out completely or in the opposite direction to that normally induced, depending on the direction and strength of the cross-wind. To safeguard against ground-loops on landing a strict limit of 10 knots maximum cross-wind component is imposed for all Spitfires and 15 knots for the Lancaster.

The newly qualified Spitfire pilot will complete a full season of display flying on the Hurricanes and small Spitfires before being allowed to fly the Griffon-powered Spitfire Mk19s. Many display spectators will have noticed that propellers on Griffon-powered Spitfires rotate in the opposite direction to those of the Merlin-powered ones. For the pilot this means that

swings will tend to be opposite to each other, so he must remember which type he is flying and make absolutely sure that he has set the rudder trim in the correct sense during pre-take-off checks — fully wound forward in Merlin Spitfires and fully back in the Griffon Spitfires.

It is very difficult, of course, to maintain old aircraft in flying condition and there is absolutely no point in feeding a stores reference number into the RAF's computer at Hendon when a spare part is urgently required as about the only reply one is likely to receive is 'World War II Aircraft'.

For minor bits and pieces on the airframe side it is sometimes possible to exchange parts from 'gate guardians' at various stations, or even from the static aircraft in the two RAF Museums at Hendon and Cosford. There are still several civil Spitfires flying, but only one Hurricane, and a bit of 'horse-trading' does go on between interested parties from time to time.

All recovery attempts of war-time crashes are automatically reported to BBMF by the Ministry of Defence department responsible for such matters, but it is only rarely that anything reusable is obtained from such 'digs'. A much more fruitful source of supply is from firms who advertise in various technical and flying journals and the For Sale columns are always religiously perused. It is quite surprising that, all these years later, there is so much wartime equipment still being offered for sale, much of it is electrical gear which one would have supposed to have long ago been sold for purposes other than aviation.

The number of Merlin engines held in reserve to replace time-expired ones in BBMF aircraft has gradually reduced over the years and was causing a little concern until recently, when a new batch was obtained. These had been produced in France under licence and had orginally been destined for the Spanish Air Force which, at one time, used them to power their Me 109s and He 111s — it's a small world, as they say! However, the Griffon engine, as fitted to two BBMF Mk 19 Spitfires, is definitely in short supply, but Rolls-Royce is working on a modification to turn the contra-prop Griffon, as fitted in Shackleton aircraft, into a single-prop one; it will take some time due to a number of complications. Despite all, the BBMF servicing team usually manages to produce the required aircraft on the day even if one of two do not 'look quite right somehow' to the experts.

One such case during the 1977 display season occurred when it was necessary to fit a four-bladed Spitfire propeller to a Hurricane for the first time. The

Right: A fine air-to-air shot by David Davies of the PR Spitfire XIX PM631. / *Air Portraits*

Hurricane's performance was actually improved, so perhaps if this had happened during the Battle of Britain the RAF's greatest victory might have been more emphatic. Another case is that for a number of years now the Lancaster has been fitted with Hastings wheels, which have a smaller diameter than the original Lancaster ones.

BBMF receives (almost needless to say) tremendous support from other RAF units and the British aircraft industry. At times is is quite startling to note the enthusiasm that can be generated when a straightforward request to a firm or organisation is made and the observation is added 'that it is to try and keep a Lancaster/Hurricane/Spitfire airworthy'. It is impossible in this short article to name all the sources of help received by BBMF over the years, but two examples might give an insight into some of the behind-the-scenes activity that goes on in addition to the more obvious sources.

The first case concerned the fitting of the mid-upper turret to the Lancaster. For many years the RAF had let it be known that they were in urgent need of a mid-upper turret to bring the Lancaster back to its wartime configuration. It was a Warwickshire businessman who first spotted one on his travels — but that was in the Argentine, a country whose air force had operated Lancasters and Lincolns in the early post-war years. The Royal Navy came to the rescue when they transported it back to England on board HMS *Hampshire* after it had been presented to the RAF. It

Above: Lancaster B1 *City of Lincoln* representing 617 Sqn past keeping company with Vulcan B1 XL317 of 617 Sqn present in May 1977. / *Air Portraits*

Above right: The Memorial Flight Spitfire Vb AB910, carrying 92 Sqn markings, and Hurricane LF363 with DH Mosquito HT-E at the first Duxford display weekend. / *Austin J. Brown*

was some time before it could be fitted to the Lanc, however, as the fairing which surrounds it on the top fuselage had to be hand-made. That presented two problems, finding a firm that could undertake such a task and providing funds to pay for it, as the RAF, quite rightly, will only spend the very limited amount of money available on essential items required to keep historic aircraft in flying condition. That situation came to the notice of the Lincolnshire Lancaster Committee which not only provided the necessary funding but also found a firm — Mariner Engineering Ltd of Grimsby — who, after making a first-class job of building and fitting the fairing, submitted a bill which must have represented only a fraction of the true cost to that firm.

The chairman of the Lincolnshire Lancaster Committee at that time, incidentally, was Mrs Hilda Buttery who had become famous towards the end of 1973 by presenting a petition, signed by over 20,000

people, to the Minister of Defence requesting that the Lancaster be returned to Lincolnshire as soon as possible. This took place shortly after the Lancaster had left Waddington to join the BBMF in Norfolk. That indicated, possibly better than anything else could, the high esteem in which the Royal Air Force was, and still is, held in the county of Lincolnshire, the county in which a very high percentage of the Lancasters of Bomber Command were based during World War II.

The second example concerns a retired engineer who had seen RAF service during the war and had become something of a Merlin expert. His main interest nowadays is steam locomotives but for old time's sake he came to the RAF Coningsby Open Day of 1977. After noting that the pilot of the Lancaster had had to 'feather' one of the engines during the display he immediately volunteered to help in the rectification work. He stayed and worked extremely hard for five days. The BBMF have ever since been extremely grateful to Mr Ken John of Diss, Norfolk, not only for helping to get the Lancaster flying again just in time to make the Paris Air Show of that year, but also for demonstrating the wartime dedication of RAF ground personnel to many airmen who were not born until long after the end of that bitter conflict. In fact, an example to us all in this day and age.

The only established members of the Flight, that is to say the only members who work full time on the BBMF, are 10 technical experts of various trades and rank. They range from one chief technician who is NCO i/c, and always a piston-engine expert, down to a number of junior technicians. The life led by these NCOs and junior technicians probably varies more than that of any other body of men serving in today's Royal Air Force. During the non-display months of October to April they are working flat-out (and that means a lot of overtime hours in the evenings in addition to the normal day) on minor inspections on all the historic aircraft left at Coningsby. On average, two of the historic aircraft will be flown, at the end of each September, to RAF Kemble for major inspections.

During the display months of May to September the servicing team will be working away from base almost every weekend at various locations in the UK and Western Europe. Depending on the location of each display they will find themselves living in accommodation that can range from a good five-star hotel, through the familiar RAF standard at operational stations, to being invited to sleep on camp beds in derelict buildings at long-abandoned airfields. The latter type of accommodation is declined whenever possible but although the RAF does expect, and provides funds for, a reasonable standard of accommodation, it is often too late at the end of a long day's flying for one of the aircrew officers to tour the countryside looking for vacant hotel rooms.

Despite the strains on family life of being away from home almost every weekend during the summer, the long working hours and the inevitability of spending more money when away from home than one would normally do, morale is remarkably high among the members of the BBMF servicing team and there has never been a shortage of vounteers to fill any position that becomes vacant. This is a classic case of morale nearly always being higher on smaller units but particularly so on those that are subjected to prolonged hard work.

The BBMF is involved in approximately 120 displays of one form or another during a typical display season. No two displays are alike; they range from straight fly-pasts by the three historic types (Lancaster, Spitfire and Hurricane) in vic formation over a particular outdoor exhibition, which in some cases is completely unconnected with aviation, to performing on a number of consecutive days at such world famous air displays as Farnborough or Paris. On some occasions only one aircraft will be involved, the type often being dictated by the event which might well be to commemorate some personage or historic action.

But how does the BBMF decide at what events they will perform? The quick answer is that they don't. What the BBMF is responsible for, however, is making absolutely sure that it never exceeds the number of flying hours that have been specified by the Ministry of Defence for a particular year. The total laid down is not only for display flying but is to include all monthly training, conversions to type and practice displays. The actual number of hours allocated has been fairly static in recent years and works out at a combined total of 200 hours for all six Spitfires and Hurricanes and 55 for the Lancaster. The two most important aspects considered before arriving at a decision on the number of flying hours allowed are, firstly; financial prudence, which is obviously of great importance, and, secondly; the desire to prolong the life of these great aircraft well into the future.

But who does finally decide what display teams will, or will not, be seen at your local air show? In the case of the Royal Air Force, and at the end of the line upwards, it will be a member of the Air Force Board who will agree, or otherwise, detailed plans submitted by a body known as the Participation Committee. This committee, after receiving a broad outline of what is thought possible for the next display season from a MoD Department called S4D (more about that later), will seek expert advice from a number of other departments before drawing up those detailed plans. Some of the departments that are always consulted, and for very obvious reasons, are the RAF Inspectorate of Recruiting, MoD Public Relations and the National Air Traffic Services. But to go back to the activities of S4D. It requires that all bids for the participation of any RAF aircraft, single aircraft as

well as display teams, reach it by 1 November of each year. This date might, at first sight, seem a little early but it is RAF policy to have the final display programme approved and distributed by the middle of February for that particular year. The mid-February deadline is solely for the convenience of display organisers who have a tremendous amount of detailed planning to get through, often in their spare time, to ensure the success of any air display. After recording all the bids, two members of S4D will visit not only all the major RAF teams such as the Red Arrows, Vintage Pair, Falcons, BBMF and Bulldogs but also the group HQ that controls and supplies the single operational types that are always in great demand and nearly always include, to name but a few, Vulcans, Harriers, Buccaneers, Jaguars and last, but certainly not least in demand, the tactical and air sea rescue helicopters. During these visits some very basic decisions will be made as to what is possible for the following season. Other decisions are deferred until a meeting of representatives of all the teams, stations, groups and command HQ in December, after which firm proposals are submitted to the Participation Committee.

There are only a very few clear-cut decisions as to what air show should have priority over another when there is a clash of dates. The two most obvious ones, however, are Farnborough and Battle of Britain Day stations, but Greenham Common and Woodford are of equal importance as all profits go to the Royal Air Force Benevolent Fund and the Royal Air Force Association respectively from these two displays. To try and be fair to all concerned when sorting out other bids is a difficult and time-consuming task. Some factors that must be considered are very basic, such as how many spectators are likely to attend a particular display. How many air displays are due to take place in that part of the UK and how many have they had in the past two or three years? One factor that is not as straightforward as it might seem is the distance from the base airfields of the various displays. Let us take the case of the BBMF operating from Lincolnshire. If bids of equal merit are submitted from an airfield in Yorkshire and from one in Cornwall for a particular Saturday it might seem obvious to agree the Yorkshire bid due to the few precious flying hours involved compared with a round trip to Cornwall. However, if the following Monday was a public holiday and four or five bids had been received from south coast resorts which could be fitted in on the return flight from Cornwall then it would be the Cornwall bid that would win the day.

Life is never that simple, however, and sometimes it is a case of should the BBMF be committed to five displays in the west, or four in the east over a particular weekend. The weather factor, if nothing

Above: PA474 pictured before installation of the mid-upper turret. *Austin J. Brown*

else, would certainly favour the east and so arguments for and against a particular combination of displays do tend to go on a bit before the inevitable compromise is reached. One can only feel sympathy for the gentlemen of S4D, for air displays are only a very small part of the total commitment of that department. As already stated, by mid-February the die will be cast with the publication of the RAF's Air Participation Programme for that year. It is then up to the HQ staffs controlling the various teams and individual aircraft to try and reach an agreement with individual display organisers on the actual timing of particular display items. To take the BBMF again, if they have only one display on for a particular day timing will be of little or no importance. However, if they have to give three of four displays it is important that the first·one starts early in that programme so that BBMF can press on to the next venue.

The second and subsequent displays must have timings that are related to the transit flying times between the various displays and, sadly, it is sometimes necessary to cancel a particular display at very short notice because of this factor. There are two very simple reasons for this situation so let us give, as an example, a flight that involves displays at A, B, C and D. Everything has been timed for a landing at D two hours after taking off from A. The flight might be

running very smoothly until the formation is approaching C when, over the R/T, comes the call 'will you hold off for 10 minutes we are running late?' The reply, however reluctantly given, is nearly always to the effect that the display will have to be given on time or not at all. As you will have probably guessed, the two reasons for declining are that it would be irresponsible to disrupt the programme at D by arriving late, and, secondly, all aircraft have a safe time that they can remain airborne depending on fuel carried. Even will full tanks, two hours is about the limit for Spitfires and Hurricanes when factors such as diversions and weather are considered. On any cancellation, however, and for whatever reason, the crews will feel just as badly about it as the spectators and the get-together of ground and aircrews at the end of the day will not be the same as it would have been at the end of a completely successful day.

At least twice during any year three historic aircraft of the BBMF will be away from Coningsby for a week of more, although some of the aircrews will return to their home stations to resume normal duties. They, or replacement crews, will return to start the next session of display flying the following weekend. It might be of more interest to readers to describe one such detachment during the 1977 display season rather than concentrate on just one weekend's flying.

The reason for deciding to leave the aircraft away from base for a full week at the end of August 1977 was that the last display of the Bank Holiday weekend was to be at Weston-super-Mare on the Monday, and the start of the next weekend's flying was to be at the Royal Naval Air Station, Yeovilton, which is only a few miles away from Weston. It would, of course, have been a nonsense to bring the aircraft back to Lincolnshire on a Tuesday only to return them to

Somerset on the following Friday and, thereby, use up about 10 precious flying hours on non-productive flying.

It was about mid-day on that particular August Sunday when the aircrew started to report to the BBMF for what might have proved to be a particularly demanding day, but the weather, at least, was near perfect for display flying. The servicing team had already been on duty for a good two hours before that getting the Lancaster, Spitfire and Hurricane out of the hangar, checking the fuel loads, carrying our full pre-flight inspections on each aircraft and storing spares and personal belongings of air and ground crews due to travel in the Lancaster.

However, BBMF personnel were not the only people working on that particular holiday Sunday at Coningsby. Without the manning of the control tower, operations room, fire section, signals traffic, telephone exchange, catering section (for early pre-flight meals) and, possibly most important of all, met office, the historic aircraft would not have been flying on that, or any other, day.

The services of the met office are, of course, of particular value to aviation but never more so than when used by operators of historic and irreplaceable aircraft. This is due to the strict weather limits that these aircraft are allowed to operate under plus the fact that very few of them have ever been fitted with airframe anti-icing equipment. The limits used by the BBMF are a minimum cloud base of 1500ft above the highest ground to be flown over, a visibility of 5km or more for the entire route and, as already mentioned, a maximum cross-wind component of 10 knots across any runway that might be used. It follows from the cross-wind ruling that airfields that have more than one runway are far less demanding than single-runway ones.

When BBMF aircrew visit the met office about two hours before take-off, the duty forecaster has not only to give his professional opinion on what the weather is likely to be over Coningsby for the duration of the proposed flight, but also for the entire route and a number of diversion airfields.

After the Met conference, a thorough briefing is given by the formation leader, and that in most cases means the Lancaster captain, on the proposed route to be flown; the height, speed and join-up procedure after take-off plus the actual timings at each display venue and the amount of time each individual aircraft of the formation will stay on display. Other factors that must be considered at the briefings are the action to be taken in the event of radio failure in any one aircraft, the action the entire formation will take if the weather falls below limits en route, and various emergency situations that might arise. All crews and passengers due to fly in the Lancaster proceed to the aircraft 45 minutes before take-off.

The Lancaster can carry a total of nine people, the first four positions being taken by the operating crew of captain, co-pilot, navigator and flight engineer. The five extra places are usually filled by members of the servicing team. If more than five ground crew are required for a particular display venue, and this largely depends on whether it is an active RAF airfield or not, the extra members will be transported in a Devon aircraft provided by 207 Sqn from Northolt. The reason for air travel is that the entire servicing team must be available to work on the BBMF aircraft as soon as they arrive at the first landing field to refuel and rectify any minor snags.

After arriving at the Lancaster the captain and flight engineer will start pre-start checks of the outside and inside of the aircraft, taking about 20 minutes; a further five minutes will be spent on strapping in and making sure everything is ready for starting the engines. Then comes starting the four engines, which takes about five minutes. On the average airfield five minutes is allowed for taxying to the take-off point and another five minutes will be required for running up and testing the engines, which is carried out by exercising two at a time in symmetrical pairs. The last five minutes before take-off is used to complete the pre-take-off checks. The Lancaster will always use the full take-off run available, whereas the Spitfire and Hurricane, which need only a very short distance, will turn on to the runway at any convenient point that might present itself. One important reason for this, apart from trying to avoid brake overheating that is likely when taxying over long distances on hot days, is that the Merlin liquid-cooled engine when fitted to fighter-type aircraft with comparatively small radiators will eventually boil if the aircraft does not get airborne within a certain time. The time will depend to a large extent on the ambient temperature. The Lancaster, flying at lower speeds than the fighters, was designed with a far bigger radiator and, consequently, does not have the same problem on the ground. If everything goes according to plan the three aircraft will be lined up on the runway ready to take off at the appointed time.

The Spitfire and Hurricane take off in formation, the one on the down-wind side leading if there should be a cross-wind so that the slipstream will be blown away from the other aircraft rather than into it; the Lancaster follows 30 seconds later. Shortly after take-off the two fighters complete a 360deg turn, one to the right and the other to the left, after which they should be in a good position to join formation on the Lancaster. It is usual for the Hurricane to join on the starboard and the Spitfire on the port side. After the Lancaster has been carefully lined up on the centre of the runway all engines are opened up to −2lb of boost before releasing the brakes. After this it is necessary for the pilot to lead with the port throttles as he opens up to +9lb of boost to try and counteract the tendency to swing to port. By leaving the control column in the central position the tail will lift by itself at about 50 knots and then the swing can be corrected by rudder. At about 70 to 80 knots a slight backward movement of the stick will lift the Lancaster off the ground. The brakes are then applied and the undercarriage lifted. At 130 knots the power is reduced from +9 and 3000rpm to +4 and 2650rpm. The 20deg of flap that is always set for take-off is retracted at 300ft, at which point the aircraft will sink a little before climbing away. The formation normally flies at 2000ft and 150 knots during transit flights. Many pilots have said over the years that the Lancaster is just like a big Tiger Moth to fly and that just about sums it up as there can be very few, if any, other aircraft of the size of the Lancaster that are so pleasant to fly. The only real difficulty is landing in a cross-wind when, apart from the aircraft tending to swing, the into-wind wing tends to lift to alarming angles if prompt corrective action is not taken. As well as the light and effective controls, the view from the large perspex-enclosed cockpit (known to all as the glasshouse) is extremely good and far superior to what is ever possible in today's pressurised aircraft.

The first turning point after take-off on the Sunday being described was to be Lincoln Cathedral, said by many to be the second most beautiful in England but, when seen from the air on a good day, often taking the top rating from aviators. Just short of Lincoln the Spitfire pilot called up to say that his engine was 'running rough' and he was returning to base. Although a reserve Spitfire was available, time would not permit the pilot to reach Coningsby, change aircraft and then catch up with the formation. After passing over Lincoln the Lancaster and Hurricane flew on to the north for another six miles before turning to the west, after passing over Scampton, which is still the base of 617 Sqn, as it was when they mounted the most famous Lancaster raid of World War II and became known from then on as The Dambusters. The route to the west had a deliberate, or known, error built in as the first display venue can be a little difficult to find in anything but very good visibility. It is place called Crich in the Derbyshire Dales and is the home of a Tramway Museum.

It is, however, one of the best places from which to view an air display as the spectators are gathered on the side of a hill and can look down on the aircraft at times as they fly up and down the valley below. The deliberate error was built in so that when the formation reached a certain railway line a turn to starboard would point the aircraft up the correct valley and, believe me, all valleys look alike in that part of the world! With the loss of one aircraft all display timings for the remaining two had to be adjusted. This task was carried out by the Lancaster navigator and passed over the R/T to the Hurricane pilot.

After the Crich display a course of almost due south was set as the next one was to be at Leicester Airport. The direct track would have taken the formation right through the East Midlands Control Zone at Castle Donington so an extra 10 minutes had been added to the flight plan time to allow for a route to the west of it. In the event, a delightful lady air traffic controller invited us to fly right through as there was 'very little traffic at that time'. It is always a pleasure to fly directly over a civil airfield as it can almost be guaranteed that there will be many people on the ground who will look up and think about the days when they flew or worked on some of the most famous aircraft of all time. The extra 10 minutes now in hand had to be lost so a number of orbits over a disused airfield were made and it was during these orbits that the Harvard and B-17, which were on the Leicester programme immediately before the BBMF, were sighted. The B-17 is the only one flying in the UK and is operated by an aircraft ferry firm called Euroworld. The actual display at Leicester is always particularly well organised and everything went without a hitch. After leaving Leicester the formation set course for the East of England Showground, on the outskirts of Peterborough. Once again a direct track was not possible as a small civil airfield not far from Peterborough was due to have 'parachute jumping in progress' and so it proved. The display area itself is a little difficult to perform over as there is no obvious 'display line' as there is on an airfield, when the runway itself is normally used. Another feature of this particular venue is the very tall road lamp standards which call for extra caution and hence an increase in height.

That was the third and final display for the day but the next day was also to be a three-display day and of slightly longer duration, which made it imperative that an airfield near the location of the first venue, the small north-Norfolk town of Aylsham, be used for an overnight stay. The RAF Station at Coltishall is only a few miles from Aylsham but rather than open up that station just for a few minutes for the landing, and again for the take-off the next day, it was decided to approach the authorities at Norwich Municipal Airport to see if the BBMF could use their airport. As always, the utmost co-operation was extended by the airport management and also by the staff of that particularly friendly airline which is resident at Norwich — Air Anglia. Fuel for the aircraft and accommodation for the crews was to be provided by

RAF Coltishall and everything was on hand when the Lancaster and Hurricane landed after a flight of just over two hours. Shortly afterwards the relief Spitfire, flown by the Coningsby Station Commander, landed so that the next day's flying would see the BBMF with the usual three-ship formation. In the particularly wet summer of 1977 it was unusual to have two consecutive fine days but the Monday proved to be another good flying day. The take-off from Norwich was left to the last possible minute as the fighters would only have fuel left for a diversion to Lyneham if a landing at Weston should prove impossible for any reason. However, the entire flight went like clockwork. The display at Aylsham was a little difficult but only on account of the close proximity of the display site to the town and the wish of the aircrew to cause as little inconvenience with engine noise as possible.

The second display that day was also a non-airfield site, at Tewkesbury in the Severn Valley. This meant a long transit flight across the centre of England which took in the Fens and the Cotswolds. It was a beautiful day and England could not have looked better. For the Lancaster crew, relaxed during the long non-deviating flight, there was the added advantage of seeing the beautiful lines of the Spitfire and Hurricane in flight. There is usually something that is completely unexpected during a display and at Tewkesbury it was a helicopter that suddenly took off from the display area as the BBMF was running-in that caused a little stir in the Lancaster cockpit. It only lifted a few feet, and there was absolutely no danger, but it did cause a momentary distraction. After rejoining formation, the BBMF proceeded down the Severn Valley in a near cloudless sky but there was still just one problem left and that concerned the Weston-super-Mare airfield with its rather limited runway length. Although the length is quite adequate for Spitfires and Hurricanes it requires a wind of 10 knots down the runway to make it absolutely safe for the Lancaster to land. In the event, the slight westerly wind had been reinforced by a sea breeze by the time the BBMF arrived and it had got up to a respectable 12-15knots but, even so, the Lancaster was put very firmly down just after the start of the runway without any attempt at a prolonged 'hold-off' and smooth touchdown.

Weston poses quite a few problems for the groundcrew due to the fact that all refuelling is carried out from a static pump and the Spitfire and Hurricane have to be manhandled to that point. Ground electrical power can also pose a problem as the Spitfires need 12 volts for starting and the Lancaster 24 volts and it is only rarely that both are readily available at the small civil airfields. BBMF tradesmen are never lost for long and the joining up, or disconnecting of batteries to get the right voltage is a fairly familiar chore. Another item that is often in short supply nowadays is compressed air and even when it is available the connections are usually of the wrong type. An amazing number of connecter/adapters are, therefore, always carried aboard the Lancaster when BBMF aircraft are due to land away from Coningsby.

It was quite late in the evening by the time all after-flight servicing had been carried out and the two fighters had been put into a hangar for the night. Although all air and ground crews had beds booked at RAF Locking it was decided that all should have a meal together in down-town Weston followed by a few drinks back at the Flying Club. It was one of the better nights for the BBMF as the Weston Flying Club is a particularly friendly place and there are always interesting people to meet there. There was no point in rushing around the next morning as the only task was to position the aircraft at Yeovilton, which would involve a 10-minute flight only. The decision to leave at about 10.30hrs proved to be just about right as there was still a little low stratus hanging around as the take-off time arrived. As always there was a particularly warm welcome at Yeovilton and the crews of the Navy's own historic flight, which is based there, were to be our hosts for the next four days.

About half of the BBMF aircrew returned to their home stations immediately after arriving at Yeovilton but the replacement crews had to arrive by the Thursday as the BBC wished to carry out some filming in connection with a production dealing with the 60th Anniversary of the Royal Air Force. This was followed by a Press Day on the Friday but there was still ample time to view the Royal Naval Air Museum which must, surely, be one of the best in the world and a visit should be a must for aviation enthusiasts who happen to take their holidays in the West Country. The Saturday of Yeovilton's Open Day was another particularly good flying day with almost unlimited visibility and a steady 10 knot wind straight down the runway. The BBMF was due to demonstrate quite early in the programme as we were also to perform at RAF Binbrook the same afternoon.

It was during the morning of that Saturday that an officer from Coningsby rang to say that his daughter was to be married in the Parish Church at Market Deeping, just north of Peterborough, and was there any chance at all of flying over it during out transit to Binbrook. The navigator of the Lancaster said that it was only one mile to starboard of his planned track and that would present no problems. However, the timings at the two air displays had to be met and an estimated time of arrival over the church was passed to the proud father.

But back to the Yeovilton Air Display; 15 minutes had been allocated to the BBMF and that included the take-off and form up. Allowing for the run-in and break and rejoining, plus the 'time-on' for the Spitfire and Hurricane, the Lancaster was left with only four minutes for its solo performance which, in effect, means only two runs along the crowd-line. It was decided to do one fast low run, which is carried out 'clean' and is flown at 200 knots and no lower than 100ft ACL, and one slow run which is flown with undercarriage down, bomb doors open and at about 90 knots. After the last run the formation was asked to reform for a final low fly-past and departure to the north-east. During the last run the message 'Fly Royal Air Force' was flashed on the aldis lamp by the Lancaster co-pilot; there was no reply from polite Yeovilton but when the same message was sent to a Royal Navy frigate as the Lancaster approached Jersey a few weeks later there was an instant, and typical, RN reply which, unfortunately, is unprintable!

The long flight to RAF Binbrook in Lincolnshire was fairly uneventful but no matter how long one has been flying with the BBMF one never quite gets used to the interest that the passing of the formation causes on the ground. Everybody seems to look up, cars often come to a sudden stop and people jump out to get a better view — once one was even seen to leave the road; bowlers have been seen to stop their run-up to the wicket — perhaps even dropped catches could be

blamed on the BBMF! What the aircrew aboard the Lancaster did not really expect to see that day, however, was the entire wedding party outside the church at Market Deeping standing in good viewing positions. It was highly improbable that the wedding was just about to start, or finish, at such a random time as 15.20hrs. This assumption was correct, it was the vicar of that church who was as keen as anybody else to see a Spitfire, Hurricane and Lancaster fly over in formation and he had delayed the start of the wedding service until after the fly-past.

One thing about any air display is that one is never quite sure who one is going to meet after landing from another airfield. At Binbrook it was noted that no lesser persons than the new AOC of No 11 Group, (AVM Peter Latham, himself one of the best formation aerobatic leaders ever, when he was with 111 Sqn), who controls the BBMF, and the Station Commander from RAF Scampton, who had most of the Lancaster crew under his command, who were taking a keen interest in the standard of flying and the deportment of aircrew as the after-flight de-brief took place.

That night in the RAF Binbrook mess was particularly interesting as it is not very often that aircrew who have just taken part in a display will hear what the local organisers thought of it all. This particularly applies when one overhears views on one's own part in it — if it is complimentary, that is!

Next morning, another Sunday by this time, the BBMF was airborne again by about 10.00 for a flight to Waterbeach to take part in an air display organised by the Burma Star Association. For anybody with connections with the 14th (Forgotten) Army it should be noted that this is an annual event and takes place on the first September Sunday of each year. The track from Binbrook to Waterbeach passed right over the base airfield at Coningsby and it felt a little strange to look down on it and wonder what the rest of the people on the station were doing that Sunday morning. The term a 'special breed' has probably been over-used over the years but that is the only way to describe the 14th Army men that attend this annual get together. Always smart, quiet, unassuming gentlemen who have retained their military bearing regardless of age. Apart from the air display there is always a very interesting military display in the main arena.

After taking off and giving the standard display, the BBMF set course for the north and home. There was just one more display before landing and that was at Holbeach St John; not a particularly well-known airfield but home to the Fenland Aero Club and, as the name implies, a little off the beaten track. It is a grass airfield and seems incredibly small from the air but all BBMF aircrew always enjoy performing there with its fairly short 'crowd line'. As night follows day, a very nice letter of appreciation always reaches the BBMF

Below: BBMF's Spitfire PM631 and Hurricane PZ865 formating near Yeovilton with three from the Fleet Air Arm Historic Flight in May 1977. / *Air Portraits*

after the Fenland display and is always greatly appreciated.

It is always nice to arrive back at base, not least because of the warm welcome that is given by many of the local population who position themselves on a public road, with the unromantic name of Dogdyke Lane, to watch the historics taxi to their hangar a few yards from the perimeter fence.

It had only been one week exactly since the BBMF had left Coningsby but it seemed a lot longer. Ten full displays had been given, crews had lived in four different messes and countless people had been met for the first time, or for the first time since the same place last year. It's a great life, however, and nobody who ever gets the taste for it will readily give it up.

From time to time people ask if any flights are more memorable than others. The ones that will always stick in my mind include a flight that took in all the main cities of Holland; a flight over the grave of Guy Gibson and his navigator, also in Holland; the 'small boats' gathering at Dunkirk; a fly-past at 500ft over London which took in Buckingham Palace; the Chadwick/Thorn memorial at the Hendon Museum exactly 45 minutes after leaving that building and having met MRAF Butch Harris and Sir Barnes Wallace; a re-enactment of the Dams Raid over the Derwent Valley exactly 34 years to the day after it took place, knowing full well that I was under the critical gaze of the survivors of that raid; and performing over RAF Scampton for past and present members of 617 Sqn, knowing that my wife was a guest of that squadron. She reported later that many of the wartime members, and that included some of the bravest of the brave, had suddenly developed colds as the Lancaster was first sighted in the distance.

One trip that should also have been included, but only for personal reasons, was the Southport Flower Show. The location was less than 400 yards from the site from which pleasure flight aircraft once operated on the famous Southport sands and that is probably how it all started for me 40 years ago, when Alan Cobham's flying circus gave me my first close-up sight of aircraft.

Lancaster B1 PA474 *City of Lincoln* was built in 1945 at Hawarden, near Chester, by Vickers Armstrong. It was undergoing modifications for use with Tiger Force in the Far East when the war ended. Later remodified for use on photo-reconnaissance work and spent six years with 82 Sqn in the Middle East and Africa on various aerial survey projects. In August 1952 PA474 was loaned to Flight Refuelling Ltd for trials. From there it moved, in March 1954, to the Royal Aircraft Establishment at Cranfield, where it was fitted with a dorsal fin for laminar-flow swept-wing flight trials. After the trials PA474 was stored at RAF Henlow until adoption by the MoD Air Historical Branch in October 1963; it was flown from Henlow to Waddington in August 1965 and was there restored and painted in standard wartime Bomber Command camouflage and given the code letters KM-B to represent the aircraft flown from Waddington by Sqn Ldr J. D. Nettleton VC of 44 (Rhodesia) Sqn, the first squadron to receive the Lancaster. In 1973 PA474 joined the Battle of Britain Memorial Flight at Coltishall and a mid-upper turret and functioning bomb doors were installed. In 1975, PA474 was adopted by the citizens of Lincoln and has since carried the Coat of Arms of that city and the name *City of Lincoln* on the front fuselage.

Hurricane Mk 11c PZ865 was the very last of about 14,000 Hurricanes to be built and came off the production line at Langley in July 1944. It was retained by the Hawker Aircraft Company at Langley and finally purchased by them in 1945. In 1950 it featured in the film *Angels One Five* after which it was converted to civil markings and registered C-AMAU. In company colours it appeared at numerous air displays in many parts of the UK until 1960, when it was once again repainted in wartime camouflage and markings prior to being put on display in the Hawker Aircraft Museum. After extensive reconditioning this Hurricane was presented by Hawkers to the Battle of Britain Memorial Flight in March 1972. The photo shows the aircraft in the letters of No 257 (Burma) Squadron (DT) and the aircraft letter (A) which

Above left: A closer view of Spitfire PR19 during a demonstration at Weston-super-Mare. *Austin J. Brown*

Above: Lancaster PA474 restored to full mission trim, about to land. *Inter-Air Press*

represents the personal aircraft letter of Wg Cdr 'Bob' Stanford-Tuck, one-time Commanding Officer of No 257.

Hurricane Mk 11c LF363 was built at Langley, Bucks, in January 1944 and saw service with 63, 309 (Polish) and 26 Sqns. After the war it continued to fly with numerous station flights and re-entered squadron service with No 41 at Biggin Hill in August 1951. LF363 stayed at Biggin Hill and joined the BBMF on its formation at that station in July 1957. It featured in the films *Angels One Five*, *Reach for the Sky* and *The One That Got Away*. This aircraft is presently wearing the markings of 242 Sqn (LE) and the aircraft letter (D) which represents the aircraft flown by Gp Capt Sir Douglas Bader who, as a squadron leader, commanded No 242 during the Battle of Britain.

Spitfire Mk 11A P7350 was built at Castle Bromwich in January 1940 and took part in the Battle of Britain, operating with No 266 (Rhodesia) Sqn from Hornchurch. Between the end of 1940 and August 1941 it served on 603 (City of Edinburgh), 616 (County of South Yorkshire) and 64 Sqns. From then until the end of the war it flew with various training units. In 1947 it was sold to Messrs John Dale who later presented it to the RAF Colerne Museum. In 1967 it was renovated for use in the making of the film *Battle of Britain*, after which it joined the Memorial Flight. P7350 is now painted UO-T of 266 Sqn, its actual markings during the Battle of Britain. Probably the oldest flying RAF aircraft.

Spitfire Mk Vb AB910 was also built at Castle Bromwich. It came off the production line in 1941 after which it saw service with 222 (Natal), 130 (Punjab), 133 (Eagle), 242 (Canadian), 416 (Canadian), 402 (Canadian) and 527 Sqns. On 4 April 1945 at No 53 OTU Hibaldstow a lady mechanic, ACW2 Margaret Horton, was holding the tail down on this aircraft during an engine-run when the pilot, Flt Lt Cox, mistakenly thought she had got off and took off and flew a complete circuit! She was unhurt and has visited the BBMF a number of times in recent years to look at 'her' Spitfire. In 1947 this aircraft was sold to a private owner who used it for racing and displays. It later came into the possession of BAC who presented it to the BBMF in 1965. Marked QJ-J, the letters of 92 Sqn, which had the highest number of kills during the Battle of Britain.

Spitfire PR Mk XIX PM631 was built in January 1945 and delivered to RAF Benson. It served on various reconnaissance flights before being modified for meteorological observation work, after which it became one of a number of aircraft that provided a daily flight for the Met Office from Hooton Park, near Birkenhead, and later Woodvale in Lancashire. It joined the BBMF at Biggin Hill in July 1957. Marked AD-C, the letters of XI (Fighter) Sqn.

Spitfire PR Mk XIX PS853 was also completed in January 1945, and then saw service with the Central Photographic Reconnaissance Unit. After the war it flew with 16 Sqn until 1950 when it joined PS631 at Hooton Park and Woodvale on met flights. In July 1957 it was flown by Gp Capt Johnny Johnson to Biggin Hill to join the BBMF on its formation. In 1960 it was decided to ground the aircraft and it was flown to West Raynham for use as a gate guardian. It was, however, kept in flying condition at that station and rejoined the Memorial Flight in May 1964. This aircraft is painted in photo-reconnaissance blue and wears no squadron markings, which is typical of 'photo' aircraft as they invariably served on flights rather than squadrons during World War II.

21

Above: The Boxkite in the air in the capable hands of the late
Neil Williams. / *Air Portraits*

The Shuttleworth Collection reaches its Half-Century

David Ogilvy

THE SHUTTLEWORTH COLLECTION was started in 1928, when the late Richard Shuttleworth acquired an early motorcar as his first item of historic transport, a Panhard Levassor of 1898. In the fifty years that have followed the scene has changed enormously but the theme has not; the idea throughout has been that every exhibit must work.

Today the Collection is known more for its aeroplanes than for its early road vehicles, although the latter include some early horse-drawn carriages, several cars built in the nineteenth century and some of the first-ever fire engines, one of which was built in 1780. These vehicles are on view every day and many thousands of visitors see them each year but, apart from appearances on the Veteran Car Club's annual run from London to Brighton and at a few rallies, they are seen in action mainly as adjuncts to the flying displays. A Crossley staff car used by the Royal Flying Corps in the 1914-18 war and a Ford Model T-based Hucks starter of the same period play significant roles in recreating the aviation scene of the time.

The aeroplanes are seen in action regularly and about ten flying displays are held each summer at the small all-grass aerodrome at Old Warden in Bedfordshire. The airfield itself, with small hangars, rural surroundings and a generally timeless atmosphere, goes a long way towards completing the total picture. One visitor said that the only sight to spoil the scene was the array of modern cars in the public car park. Unfortunately not even the Shuttleworth Collection can insist on its visitors arriving by Edwardian transport!

Although to the casual viewer Old Warden on a normal day might seem quiet and inactive, the activities 'off stage' have become quite involved. A small staff is kept very busy throughout most of the year, for as soon as a display season is over, plans are under way for a repeat performance in the following year. The work of restoring the aircraft receives more detailed treatment in chapter 3 and this is an activity that requires far more time than is available. Each aeroplane must have regular routine maintenance and any defects that are discovered must be rectified, usually without the facility of the required parts being available from stores. When a new machine makes its first public appearance on the flight line, several years of work, including a considerable depth of research, have often been put into that achievement.

Flying displays do not just happen. Dates must be decided more than a year ahead and preparations begin from then. If a function is to include demonstrations by aircraft of the Royal Air Force, the Ministry of Defence must be notified by early September of the preceding year and all applications are sifted by the Participation Committee. The display organiser is informed of the success — or otherwise

Above: David Ogilvy, General Manager of the Shuttleworth Collection, in typically busy mood, checking the aircraft serviceability situation. / *J. E. Hoad*

— of his request by late February or early March, *before* which time he has needed to prepare, print and start to circulate his publicity material. Should he send incomplete information or should he delay until all details are available? Either way he fails to satisfy some.

There are many sound reasons for preparations to be made as early as possible. A coach tour operator must plan his year's programme, so he needs flying display information before he can circulate his own plans. Clubs and societies making organised visits might wish to select their dates round the appearance of a specific aircraft; a group from Northumberland, making a once-only or at the most an annual visit, might ask for a date on which the RAF Lancaster and the Shuttleworth Collection's SE5a will be flying. They seek that information before the end of the previous year.

Posters, calendars of events and general publicity material must combine to form balances between detailed descriptions of the events to be held on specific dates and early-warning notices. The Shuttleworth Collection sends calendars free to any people who ask, but they are requested to send

stamped and addressed envelopes; more than 40,000 calendars are printed each year.

The Civil Aviation Authority must be informed of a proposed flying display. This allows certain airspace arrangements to be agreed and for a NOTAM to be issued to warn all pilots to expect unusual activities that might extend well beyond and above the everyday aerodrome traffic zone. Also, the aerodrome must be closed to all visiting aircraft during the hours of the display with a safety margin at each end.

As much administrative work as possible is carried out during the winter months and even the bare bones of the printed display programmes are under way before Christmas. A visitor pays for his programme, may or may not read it, and probably throws it away within two or three hours of obtaining it. Yet if supplies run out complaints are rife. To produce printed programmes at monthly intervals throughout the main season calls for more time and thought than can be spared, so the cover design and general information are agreed well in advance and just the centre page, with the breakdown of the display

Left: The Trust's Granger Archaeopteryx about to start engine. / *Air Portraits*

Below: Line-up of gems at Old Warden; (left) Hawker Siddeley's DH60 Moth, (right) Leisure Sport's DH82A Tiger Moth and Shuttleworth's RAF SE5A, LVG CVI and Avro 504K. / *Air Portraits*

Above: The 504K takes rather more effort to start up, hence the Hucks starter. / *J. E. Hoad*

Above right: Shuttleworth Trust's DH51 *Miss Kenya*, the untypenamed de Havilland two/three-seat precursor of the Moth, running up at White Waltham. / *J. E. Hoad*

sequence, is left to the eleventh hour. With a co-operative printer, the material can be supplied eight days before the event, the type set, a proof submitted, corrected and returned, and the finished article delivered on the day before the show. Tighter timing than this is impossible, yet it is relatively rare for there to be no cancellations or alterations during those last few days, when everything seems to happen.

The weather, of course, plays the leading role in any flying display, but even more so for a Shuttleworth event. At one time period themes were popular, but a gusty wind of only 10 knots could mean cancellation of a whole programme devoted to the Edwardian era. This could lead to gross disappointment among people who often come very long distances to see the 1912 Blackburn and the 'Magnificent Men' Boxkite in the air, only to find them tucked safely in their hangars out of the breeze, but safe for another day. As a result, specific eras may be included in a broadly based overall programme, rather than having total occupation. Naturally some people have shown disappointment, for those with particular interests could choose the dates of their visits to suit, but again we are faced with a situation that cannot be solved to the total satisfaction of everyone. Part of a published programme must be better than no display at all, so thoughts along these lines must be put to work in the early planning stages of a year's events.

It is possible to contact known enthusiasts either through their membership of the supporting Shuttleworth Veteran Aeroplane Society or in response to requests for information, but the Shuttleworth Collection, as any other private body, must attract sufficient custom to make financial ends meet, so publicity must be extended to those who are not already committed to the cause. This means a need to advertise to the world at large, carried out through a series of regular news releases to the press (which produce encouraging response rates) and through normal paid publicity in both display and classified columns. For some time the Collection has enjoyed at least its fair share of publicity as direct media news items, and this enables the advertising budget to be kept remarkably low. As the Richard Ormonde Shuttleworth Remembrance Trust is an educational charity, the more of its income that can be directed internally to the task of restoring, preserving and displaying the aircraft, the nearer one can get towards achieving the founder's aims.

Although economic necessity requires attendance by the undevoted public, the standards are set to the needs of the specialist. The person who attends a flying display to see just thrills and gimmicks will find little joy from a visit to Old Warden, but for the enthusiast or historian who wishes to see the best of aviation's past alive today, the Collection endeavours to fulfil his wishes. The programmes, though varied in content from one function to another, are balanced. A new aeroplane is not barred from participation just because it has no history behind it, for it might fit well into a planned pattern. The RAF's current primary trainer, the Scottish Aviation Bulldog, now serving with the 16 University Air Squadrons and other units, compares interestingly with, perhaps, the Avro Tutor that carried out a similar function more than 40 years earlier.

Let us jump now to the morning of an average Flying Day at Old Warden. Before 09.00 many of the aeroplanes are outside; they have been pre-flighted and signed out. Cadets from the RAF OCTU at nearby Henlow are being briefed for airfield security duties; for safety's sake only people with the correct lapel badges may enter the manœuvring area. The public must be kept behind the rope that runs *behind* the fence at the south-west end of the aerodrome. This is because the normal boundary fence at that spot is too close to the laid-down display line to conform to Ministry of Defence and Civil Aviation Authority requirements. The person in charge of ground services will be showing static exhibitors and approved sales stallholders their allotted sites.

Inside, the day's meteorological forecast is being studied. For anywhere other than Old Warden the expected weather would present few problems, but a wind possibly gusting to 18 knots and the fear of isolated showers combine to pose two fears. The lighter aircraft must be faced into wind and will need tethering; the oldest on the programme might not be able to fly and many others will not benefit if the fabric becomes wet in anything more than light rain. As a start, cockpit covers must be put on. Weighing-up the overall position, but knowing that forecasts sometimes misfire, those concerned have a few words and agree that a fairly extensive display should be possible and that full Flying Day prices can be charged. If serious doubt exists, agreement must be reached well before the gates are opened to the public to charge a reduced entry price. To be safe, though, an alternative 'wind programme' is prepared so that it can be brought into use at short notice.

It is 10.15 and a moderate queue has formed in the Biggleswade road. The gate crew, who take the money and issue the tickets (the latter an important requirement to comply with the law) are collecting their petty cash for change from the accounts office, where the police are carrying out a routine security check; to prevent vehicles from becoming bogged in, the car parkers have marked a damp patch to be avoided and now they are ready for the flood to begin. Accurate parking is essential and can make a difference of several hundreds of extra visitors who can be accommodated compared with a sloppy parking system. Fortunately the Shuttleworth crews are regulars and they know their tasks as well as any group anywhere.

A Shuttleworth pilot arrives, after a long journey on a motorcycle all the way from Bristol. Shortly after, another drives in from Lancashire. These men are carefully selected for their flying experience and ability, *and* their outlooks, with the need to appreciate the responsibilities attached to handling the world's sole surviving specimens of famous historic types. They are dedicated. They receive no pay. They give up much of their free time. Yet not one Shuttleworth pilot has ever voluntarily resigned from the flying list. It is an aeronautical 'plum' to be allowed to fly the Old Warden aeroplanes and experienced people write regularly asking to be allowed to join; but the answer is always 'no', for the number of pilots must be kept to an absolute minimum to maintain at least a touch of type continuity.

An aeroplane requires an air test. There are three pilots in the display office. All would like to do it, but no one asks. Flying is shared as fairly as possible and one man who missed the previous occasion because he was on duty in his normal job is invited to do the flight. He is considerate enought to offer it to another, but the allocation remains.

Right: Shuttleworth's 1912 Blackburn Monoplane, oldest
British aeroplane still airworthy. / *Air Portraits*

Below right: Restoration work on the Boxkite in the Old Warden
hangar. / *J. E. Hoad*

The display is due to start at 14.00, so at 12.45 all
concerned with the flying and safety sides meet in the
lecture room for a full briefing. The weather is
discussed in detail and a duty runway agreed. Does
any pilot wish to use the other strip? Yes; the pilot of
the Provost wishes to land uphill on the longer run
even though it is out of wind. The others, with slower
and directionally more sensitive machines, opt for the
shorter run that is nearly into wind. The pilot of the
1916 Sopwith Pup, the 1924 DH 51 and the 1912
Blackburn ask for wing-walkers to guide them to the
take-off position and to meet them after landing for
taxying back to the line. This is because all aeroplanes
tend to weathercock into wind and lightweight
brakeless types with tailskids cannot be controlled
directionally on other headings.

The display sequence, timing and procedure are
covered. The rules are basic, but rigid; no flying over
or towards the crowds, the buildings or the parked
aircraft; very low flying is to be avoided for it is
pointless, as only the front row of many lines of
spectators can see it. All engines must be stopped at a
slot in the middle of the display when the parachutists
are descending. The balloon crew must not venture on
to the active part of the airfield until the Pup has
landed, cleared and a flashing green is given from the
control point. Other points are discussed and a short
gap is agreed for departure of visiting aircraft that
have long distances to cover; machines fly in from
most European countries and need to land elsewhere
on the way home to clear Customs.

There is not long between briefing and the start of
the display, but the pilots have quick buffet lunches
before going to their mounts. They study the wind and
assess the best display patterns for the day's
conditions, but bearing in mind throughout that safety
must take precedence over spectacle. There is no other
Bristol Fighter; there is no other Gloster Gladiator.
No, there is no other flyable specimen anywhere in the
world and each pilot knows what that means in terms
of personal responsibility.

Shuttleworth displays start on time. At 14.00 the
Provost's wheels lift off the ground to start the show.
The Provost is aerobatic and its demonstration opens
with a loop and a roll, but experience has proved that
Shuttleworth spectators are more interested in flypasts
within reach of the range of the average camera —
cine or still. Fast runs, banked runs round the airfield
side of the enclosure perimeter and slow passes in the

28

approach configuration all keep heads well exercised. A recent check from behind the public revealed about one in five spectators watching a neat and polished aerobatic sequence, but every head followed the close runs. Over the past few years very specific practices and procedures have been developed as integral parts of the Shuttleworth scene.

The weather is proving reasonably kind and the gusts to 18 knots have not fully developed, but other problems can stand in the way of a smooth programme. One machine, its engine still warm from an essential ground run carried out at lunchtime following a need to clear some fouled plugs, refuses to start again. Unless it fires now the pilot will have insufficient time to do his checks and taxi to the holding point before the previous aircraft lands. An on-the-line decision is made to start and dispatch the machine that is due up after it, for it has a rotary engine and needs virtually no warming-up period. For just such situations, pilots are briefed to be in their cockpits at least one 'act' ahead of the scheduled sequence, so the delay is minimal. Also, the pilot of the preceding machine has noticed the starting problem and has added an additional slow fly-past as a convenient time-filler. Only by intelligent co-operation of this type can a display of historic aeroplanes, which have no radio, lead from one step to the next without embarrassing gaps. Yet a high-pressure tightly timed programme must be avoided as it would ruin the informality of the occasion. So again a compromise must reign. To achieve the essential balance between extremes of wishes and outlooks is perhaps the most important management aim, with the ever-present thought that so many people are attracted to Old Warden because it is different.

The activities behind the public eye at a Flying Day could occupy several pages, but here we must extend to other sides of the Collection's working year. Often we have heard people say that everyone must be busy on a display day, but what do people do for the rest of the time?

We must remember at all times that although the Shuttleworth Collection is part of a registered charity — the Richard Ormonde Shuttleworth Remembrance Trust — it must be run as a business. Yet to accord with the charitable status, to meet the aims of the founder and to retain the public image, commercialism or gimmickry must be seen not to be seen. There is no fairy godmother to dole out gold if times are hard and the Collection receives no financial support from the government or from any official source. This means that money remains in short supply, but this problem is offset by the operating freedom that goes with independence. The main Trust acts as an overall umbrella, but its activities range through the management or several thousands of acres, operation of an agricultural college, management of farms and the ownership of a considerable number of houses, cottages and other buildings. The Collection operates separately with its own banking and administrative arrangements and the only noticeable area of overlap between the other interests concerns ownership of the land. In short, the college or a farm may need more grazing ground when the Collection seeks to expand the aerodrome. In practice, though, this works well; recently the college handed over an area of land to permit widening of the end of the grass runway at the south-west end, in exchange for an agreement for sheep to graze the airfield in the depths of winter when fodder is hard to find.

No two days at the Shuttleworth Collection are alike, except that all are unpredictable. On some occasions there are hardly any visitors, while 24 hours later, with no apparent change in weather or other external influences, the place is fairly full. This means that the sales staff must be geared to meet any situation from an almost zero return to a pair of well-filled coaches arriving within minutes of each other on a day when none has been booked. Imagine fifty or more exuberant youngsters who have been couped up for a journey of two hours or so suddenly roaring into the shop and demanding instant attention to their enthusiastic demands. Here, of course, much depends on the attitude and ability of the teachers or other people in charge of the party. Despite clearly laid-down rules regarding a teacher's responsibilities while the party is on the Trust's property, the degree of supervision ranges from pre-visit briefing with set educational exercises for the children to carry out, to 'I will see you at the coach in two hours' and disappearing to the village pub.

Apart from any enterprise that a school, or its staff, might display, the Collection provides plenty of material for those who wish to learn. There are questionnaires for varying age groups, a young people's guide with a work programme for students to connect the descriptions of exhibits with their pictures and a very wide range of generally informative literature. This includes two grades of general guide, an educational How it Works series and booklets on each range of transport exhibits — for example one on cars, another on horse-drawn vehicles — and so on. Most of these have been produced by Wing Commander T. E. Guttery, whose life-long aviation experience dates continuously from 1912 when he joined the newly formed Royal Flying Corps.

Visitors come from all over the world; most come quite independently, pay the modest entrance fee and go round the exhibits at their own paces. An interesting and useful management exercise is to listen, incognito, to customer reaction. People have been known to walk round inside 20 minutes, find nothing to fire their interest and depart to other scenes. Most wander for about an hour and a half, delaying at the subjects that tickle their individual fancies; perhaps a man almost drools over the world's only airworthy Bristol Fighter, with real working oil falling into its drip-tray to make it so different from a dead static museum exhibit. He vows to come again to see it in the air. While he indulges in some fanciful imagination — or possibly makes a serious historical study of some aspect of aviation in the 1914-18 war — his lady companion might be deriving similar satisfaction from an item of horse brass or harness in the neighbouring carriage display. Clearly in mind is one elderly gentleman who spent a whole day studying the Collection and at close of play asked for the address of the nearest hotel, so that he could return at opening time on the following morning to spend a second whole day 'taking it in'.

Many parties take advantage of the Collection's educational service. By booking in advance — well in advance for the peak summer months — a member of the staff will meet the group and provide an explanatory talk, the coverage depending on the ages or interests of the people. Many are schoolchildren, but groups from clubs, societies, colleges and universities are not uncommon. Occasionally a party is taken on a full conducted tour, but experience has proved that this is less satisfactory than an opening talk, as on the latter there is far more scope for an individual to follow his or her own line of study.

Not only do visitors come from every spot on the globe, but inquiries arrive from an equally wide range of sources. An American amateur constructor seeks some detailed information about the fuel pressurisation system of an SE5a that he is aiming to build in reproduction form; a letter in Spanish needs to be passed to an outsider for full translation, which indicates that he is endeavouring to trace one of the last four Hurricanes to have flown with the Portuguese Air Force in the nineteen-fifties. Inquiries in Portugal had failed, but surely the Shuttleworth Collection, with its worldwide reputation, can provide the answer!

A retired air marshal and a Russian schoolgirl share one interest, by both being members of the supporting Shuttleworth Veteran Aeroplane Society. This organisation is open to all who wish to back the aims of the Collection. Members receive advance publicity about events and detailed information about restoration plans and programmes; they have free access to the hangars on normal days and concession entry facilities for special events. On such days those who arrive early enough may use a special parking and viewing facility that is retained solely for their use.

Then there are the people who see the Shuttleworth Collection as a fitting home for their treasured aeronautical or transport possessions. Early aviation books and periodicals, maps, flying clothing, instruments and models are offered regularly. The librarian vets all these items carefully and is pleased to accept all those that fit into the overall Shuttleworth pattern. Occasionally large items are offered, one of the most significant in recent times being the de Havilland DH 60G Gipsy Moth G-ABAG, presented by Mrs Hull in memory of her late husband. This was received as a very welcome addition to the range of exhibits, but occasionally items cannot be accepted. A Miles Messenger and a Luton Minor are examples. These aircraft, historic though they are, needed very extensive structural attention and the management felt it unfair to the prospective donors to accept machines that might need to wait several years before being fed into the planned restoration programme. Here, though, the Collection wears its broader hat, and either aims to have the item placed with a suitable museum or arranges for it to be offered on a national basis through the British Aircraft Preservation Council. This entirely voluntary organisation is the recognised 'sifting ground' for ideas, offers and placings.

How big is the Shuttleworth Collection? It is impossible to quote a precise number of exhibits, and

Below: Acceptance at Old Warden of DH60G Gipsy Moth G-ABAG from Mrs Hull. / *J. E. Hoad*

even the number of aeroplanes, for when does a series of component parts qualify to be called an aeroplane? Clearly a tailplane and an undercarriage leg fail to comply, but what of a fuselage and one wing? Legally the identity lives with the fuselage, so some owner with a claimable registration may say that he owns that machine; but the Shuttleworth Collection has three Magister fuselages, answering to P6382 (the complete and flyable specimen) G-AIUA and G-ANWO. It would be hypocritical, though, to claim to have a flight of Maggies! As a broad guide, the Collection feels that it has an aeroplane if it owns more than 60% of the main structure and considers completion of a recognisable machine to be a practical possibility. On this basis there are about 40 aeroplanes, 26 of which are on view publicly or sufficiently complete to be exhibited. At any time though, some are always out of sight in the workshops.

On the human side there are 24 paid people on strength. At a quick count this may sound a sizeable staff for an out-of-the-way rural collection; but split this between engineering (aircraft and vehicles), sales and reception, library and research, maintenance and cleanliness of buildings and the aerodrome, accounts, secretarial and overall administration, and the mixture is spread rather thinly. Remember too, that the Collection is open to visitors on seven days each week throughout the year and participates in events and meetings in many other places; then the work allocation may begin to show through in perspective.

An important factor in the total management plan is that the Shuttleworth Collection is unique. In part it is a museum; in larger part it is a fleet of flyable aeroplanes that must be made and kept serviceable; in part it is an operator of a general-use aerodrome; in part it is a general transport collection; and its function must be largely educational. This calls for representation on a wide range of associations covering these grossly differing interests and outlooks. In combined form they are very time consuming, but in return there is a feedback of communication that is essential to the operation of the place.

The key, though, is the aim of the founder; Richard Ormonde Shuttleworth insisted that his possessions must work. Most of the effort at Old Warden is based on this aim. A clinically clean display of aeroplanes that appear artificially new may appeal to the purist historian who sees them solely as three-dimensional versions of textbook pictures; to the more enlightened individual who combines an interest in aviation history with the desire to encounter the sight, sound and even the smell of an early flying machine in action, the real oil in the driptrays brings a reminder of the life that lies under the cowlings, even when an aeroplane is sitting statically on exhibition in its hangar. That, surely, is what the Shuttleworth Collection is all about.

Below: The Trust's Spitfire V AR501. / *Air Portraits*

Keeping Historic Aircraft Flying

David Ogilvy

Each year the problems of maintaining historic aeroplanes in flying condition increase. It is clear that in future we cannot expect the machines of the Shuttleworth Collection to be available as if by magic. Here David Ogilvy explains a few of the many difficulties.

A LONG STORY lies behind almost every historic aeroplane that is to be seen flying today. Visitors to a flying display organised by the Shuttleworth Collection at Old Warden Aerodrome, near Biggleswade in Bedfordshire, might well be forgiven for failing to realise the hidden truth that lies behind the scene. It appears — and is intended to appear — so casual; as though it has all just happened without plan or effort. The hangar doors were opened, the aeroplanes wheeled out, their fuel and oil checked and

there they are ready for the pilots to climb aboard and go. How easy it all seems! To place the picture in true perspective, though, let us take a look at what really happens.

Nearly every aeroplane that has arrived at Old Warden has been out of action for a considerable time. When it comes, not only are many parts beyond practical repair, but usually several fundamental items are missing. Most probably the aircraft is the world's only surviving specimen of its type, so spares are unavailable and neither drawings nor patterns can be found. This calls for some head scratching and large measures of technical initiative.

Some problems — such as the need for time and money in large doses — may be common to every restoration project, but in the main each task sets a fresh series of posers. When the German LVG CVI,

which had seen action against the British in 1918, was being restored after more than 30 years of storage, an outside observer might have seen it as a complete if rather tired aeroplane; but it was not so to anyone whose job was to make it fit to fly again. The entire cooling system for its large Benz six-cylinder water-cooled engine was missing; research produced few ideas, but eventually a 1919 issue of *Flight* magazine revealed a line sketch, little larger than a postage stamp, from which the entire system was 'designed' and built. When the time came for flying, it boiled on the first test, but by a series of in-the-field modifications on a trial-and-error basis an acceptable operating temperature was achieved.

The same aeroplane produced numerous other problems. A main air intake scoop was missing, but to produce the right results the size and shape had to be correct. Fortunately the world could boast another LVG, hanging from a roof in Belgium, and some careful measurement enabled the existing scoop to be copied. The German colour scheme, with its lozenge pattern applied by a dye process, presented many problems to apply accurately, but within weeks of the

work being finished a young man of about eighteen years of age complained vehemently because the fabric strips on the wing ribs were of the wrong colour. When challenged, he insisted that he knew about such things, but those of us who have been close to aeroplanes in squadron service know that there may be many variations between right and wrong. Different production batches, sometimes from different factories, a repaint on the station or at a maintenance unit, often using materials that are readily available instead of waiting for the arrival of paint that matches a precise specification, can produce a small assortment of colours. This is a point that the excessive purists tend to overlook; aircraft are built and maintained to do a job of work and not just to conform to textbook paint schemes.

The fact that Shuttleworth aeroplanes still work, even if on a restricted basis in order to save them for as long as possible, provides one of their main attractions. A clinically clean and correct specimen sitting permanently in a museum might appeal to the theoretical historian, but to a person who is interested in aeroplanes as flying machines, signs of wear, with oil dripping here and there, enable them to express themselves as living things. How many visitors have noticed (certainly no one has remarked) that the wheels on the 1916 Sopwith Pup are not quite the correct size? The change from standard was not made light-heartedly, but when no tyres could be obtained and safety had to come first, new wheels were made with rims of the nearest dimensions for which tubes and covers were available.

Below left: Good buildings are essential and in 1977 Shuttleworth Trust built a new one, here seen finished and housing Gloster Gladiator L8032 and Bristol Fighter D8096. /*J. E. Hoad*

Below: Reconstruction at Old Warden of the 1934 England-Australia Air Race winner, DH88 Comet. /*J. E. Hoad*

The Pup is not alone in its problem. Literally several years of research and experiment have passed between a machine needing new covers and their arrival. This is not through lack of interest by the manufacturers, but because the moulds used in earlier times have been destroyed and non-standard sizes can be produced only on a very long-winded basis. Sometimes a cover for a road vehicle might be nearly suitable, and then the trials and tribulations begin. The treads probably need to be removed by a buffing process and even when the greatest care is taken it might be impossible to avoid damaging the structure of the tyre. When this happens, requiring the whole procedure to be started all over again, further delay is unavoidable.

There is no question of arranging for a batch of covers to be made to keep the older aeroplanes well shod for years to come. A recent count shows that twenty-six Shuttleworth aeroplanes use no fewer than fifteen sizes and in only one case is one wheel dimension shared by three machines. Despite valiant efforts by the tyre makers, the Collection's forty-year-old Gloster Gladiator single-seat fighter was very nearly grounded early in 1977 through a bald cover, although an order for a replacement set had been lodged more than three years previously. The problem was temporarily shelved, but not solved, when Vivian Bellamy, who was building a replica Sopwith Camel with a genuine Clerget rotary engine, needed a propeller. At Old Warden we had four Camel

Above: Radiator designed and built from scratch for the Benz engine of the LVG CVI. / *J. E. Hoad*

Below: Doping the fabric-covered wing of the LVG CVI after rebuild. / *J. E. Hoad*

Below right: The LVG CVI finished in original German colour scheme and ready to fly again. / *Stuart Howe*

propellers and we sent him the best, in exchange for a pair of ageing but unused Gladiator tyres that he had kept since he had restored the machine just after World War II!

This arrangement of mutual help goes a long way towards making the restoration and preservation tasks into practical possibilities. In many cases exchanges of items are organised through the British Aircraft Preservation Council, which is a purely voluntary body that holds meetings about four times a year on the premises of one of its member organisations. Exchanges of information and items are mutually beneficial and the scheme works well.

Quite often a Shuttleworth project receives help from the outside world, either in kind or in cash. The biggest commitment — and historically the most significant — has been the ambitious programme of restoring the de Havilland DH88 Comet G-ACSS *Grosvenor House*. When the Comet won the England to Australia air race in 1934 it was a daily headline hitter for a week or more; when it flies again it might well capture similarly large doses of human interest and imagination.

As an indication of the importance of the Comet project, Hants and Sussex Aviation of Portsmouth has overhauled the Gipsy Queen engines, Hawker Siddeley Dynamics has prepared the variable-pitch propellers and British Airways apprentices have provided the engine bearers, all at no expense to the Shuttleworth

Collection. This has helped very substantially towards holding the total cost of the operation to a figure lower than the price anticipated when the project was first proposed. The task was tackled after an incentive grant from the Transport Trust, which in turn was followed very quickly by a covenanted donation from the head office of Hawker Siddeley Aviation, whose Hatfield base appropriately has provided very valuable practical support from the first day.

So far, donations have kept pace with outgoings in labour and materials, but more funds will be needed soon if work is to proceed at its present pace to the point of completion. Even with more money though, a target date is impossible to forecast, for there are many variables to consider. If everything runs according to plan, 1980 is not a total impossibility, but with such a complex task several setbacks must be anticipated. The lack of one rubber seal has been known to delay a restoration for six months, so no one should express surprise if the total time needed for the Comet overruns by a year or more. When considering this, remember that nothing exists in a ready-made state, that no parts can be withdrawn from stores, that most of the original drawings are missing and that industry today is not geared to produce the types of items that are likely to be needed — and especially when required on a one-off basis.

At any moment there might be four or five aircraft in various stages of the restoration process. Usually

two or three are on the first time round after arrival at the Collection in old and tired condition, while others are going through the shops for what might be called their second helpings. Once a machine has been put into flying condition it requires a steady programme of regular continual maintenance and the clearing of running snags, but after about ten years or so much of the original process might need to be repeated. While wear and tear through flying might be minimal (very few Shuttleworth aeroplanes fly more than two or three hours in an average year) the effects of time are expensive; corrosion of metal parts, the parting of glue joints on a wooden airframe and deterioration of fabric and timber generally.

Not long ago the historic aeroplanes participated regularly at displays all over Britain and sometimes abroad. While a few 'away matches' are held today, for several reasons they have been reduced to a practical minimum. The management would like Shuttleworth aircraft to be seen globally, but with an increasing need to reduce flying time, flights between Old Warden and display sites have become too unproductive. A machine travelling for an hour or so each way to and from a display, for a public appearance of about five minutes, fails to make economic sense, so in the main the Collection's policy is to encourage spectators to come to Old Warden instead of taking the aeroplanes to the people. In some cases, certainly, there is the alternative of taking a machine by road, but experience has proved this to be damaging. Wear and tear on bushes and bolts during dismantling and assembly (remembering that each operation needs to be carried out twice) coupled with the continual shaking of the machine in transit and the fact that it might get soaked at the same time, add up to an unattractive operation that is best avoided. Clearly these problems are far more critical with a flyable aeroplane than with a static machine, which means ironically that airworthiness tends to make an older aircraft almost 'housebound'.

With a balanced fleet of historic aeroplanes, ranging from some of the world's earliest flying machines to types such as the Spitfire and those of the immediate postwar era, the Shuttleworth Collection is well placed to lay on a display wholly from local talent. Frequently other items are brought in from other places; these range from specialised aerobatic displays to fly-pasts by machines preserved by the flying Services, but the core of each event is based on the use of the unique Shuttleworth machines, which between them have an enormous world-wide following.

Just as thousands of people wish to see Old Warden's aeroplanes in action in the air, many dozens of pilots wish to fly them. To be allowed on the Shuttleworth list is quite a 'plum' in the aviation world, and regularly people with thousands of hours on

dozens of types write in with good stories to support their cases for consideration. In practice though, commonsense calls for a bare minimum of pilots, so that at least some type familiarity and continuity can be established and maintained. Clearly if an aeroplane flies only six times in a year, ideally the same person should fly it on all six occasions, but as the pilots are unpaid volunteers who travel considerable distances and who have regular jobs to do, some flexibility must be built into the system. No one pilot flies every machine and a leaning towards type specialisation helps to ensure a high standard of competence.

'Safety before spectacle' is an expression used regularly at Old Warden display briefings. The aim is not to fly an aeroplane to its limits and certainly aerobatic displays as such are right off the menu. Specific limitations are laid down for each machine and although limited aerobatic manoeuvres are permitted on some types, they do not rate highly in order of importance. A Shuttleworth aeroplane is likely to be the world's sole survivor of its type and the main idea is just to show it in its intended element — in the air. Such a sight is impossible anywhere other than at Old Warden and a main attraction for spectators is that flypasts are made just on the aerodrome side of the enclosure fence, well clear of the crowds but close enough for cameras to produce healthy results.

What is a Shuttleworth aeroplane like to fly? Obviously there is enormous difference between, as examples, the 1910 Avro Triplane and the Percival Provost of 1954, but there is a common denominator that runs through the entire operation. That is a sense of duty and an awareness of responsibility for being in charge of a very valuable and wholly irreplaceable item. This does not remove the pleasure and satisfaction to be derived from flying a unique historic machine, knowing that no one else in the world can be doing it at that time, but it stays in the front of the mind. For this reason, pilots have been selected as much for their attitudes and outlooks as for their skills and abilities.

What are the necessary skills? There is no laid-down closed-shop system in the selection process, but a broad background of flying a wide range of types must rate highly. Time cannot be spent on extensive conversion and familiarisation flying, so a pilot must be accustomed to stepping from one type to another with a minimum of difficulty. All those on the active list are former (or in two cases current) Service pilots, and all are either qualified test pilots or flying instructors, or both. Although aircraft that a military pilot may fly today differ vastly from the types at Old Warden, fortunately there are those for whom handling and airmanship standards still play leading roles.

Above: Inside view of a Spitfire, with which Old Warden maintenance crews need to be familiar. / *J. E. Hoad*

A book has been published describing the handling qualities of the various aeroplanes in the Shuttleworth Collection, so clearly a few paragraphs cannot cover the experience in detail, but perhaps the most important considerations are that wind and weather provide key factors.

In some modern types, the rudder pedals can be used as little more than movable footrests, and turns can be carried out on the control column alone, but if we move the stick in one direction on a biplane, such action could possibly result in a very unbalanced turn *the other way*. This is largely because of an increase in drag caused by the downgoing aileron, a feature that is particularly marked on types produced before the introduction of differential ailerons, on which the downward movement is considerably smaller than the upward travel of its opposite counterpart. But even with this relatively modern aid to handling, older types

generally call for extensive and accurate use of rudder in order to achieve any form of balanced flight. Flight is an unbalanced condition is not only very uncomfortable, but in a machine with a marginal performance can almost eliminate any ability to climb.

The approach and landing call for careful attention. An early adage that a good landing stems from a good and well-planned approach remains especially true with the traditional tail-dragger. If a steady trimmed-out glide approach can be established and maintained, than all available pilot attention can be devoted to

37

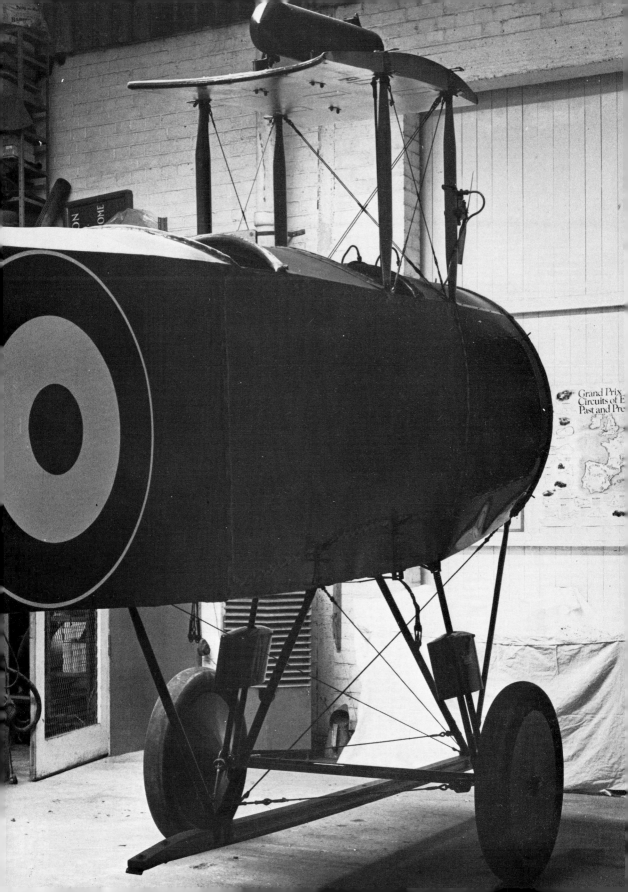

precision on the hold-off. In normal conditions the aim should be for a three-pointer, with both main wheels and the tail skid making contact together, but the job is not finished just because the aeroplane is on the ground. Quick reactions are needed to anticipate a swing before it takes hold and, from the outside, energetic rudder activity can be seen to be taking place until the machine stops.

Shuttleworth aeroplanes are demonstrated in a manner that has been built up to suit the machines and the size and shape of Old Warden aerodrome. A display pattern covering the enclosure boundaries with suitably positioned turns at each end of the runs means that the aircraft can be brought fairly close to the spectators in total safety. A run from the north-west corner (near the hangars, but *not* flying over them) gives a pilot ample flexibility to turn away into the open airfield if he should suffer the misfortune of engine trouble. A run in the reverse direction cannot provide such a sanctuary as there is no clear ground, so in general a pilot will turn into the aerodrome at the end of a run from a southerly heading and therefore retain a relatively clear path ahead.

The older slower aeroplanes are ideally suited to the confines of the Old Warden demonstration area with turning radii that fit well into the available space. After regular displays at home, though, pilots have found that vast expanses of larger aerodromes far less

Left: A stage in the restoration of the Trust's Avro 504K E3404. / *J. E. Hoad*

Below: E3404 taxying in at the end of its first flight after restoration. / *J. E. Hoad*

satisfying and, strangely, more restrictive. A long straight enclosure fence calls for a machine to take as little time as possible in moving from one end to the other, failing which there is a long and inactive gap for some of the spectators. This in turn tends to mean that long straight runs must form the basis of a display, which leads to monotony. A series of turns away from the spectators, but returning to a straight display line between each manoeuvre, helps to enliven the sequence, but also lengthens it and extends the gaps for people viewing from the enclosure extremities. Clearly large and fast aeroplanes are easier to display on large aerodromes and small slow machines are happiest in the environment that Old Warden is able to offer.

At one time, many people felt that rare historic aeroplanes should not be exposed to the risks that are inseparable from flying. However, in recent years more interesting aircraft have been damaged or destroyed through falling into uncaring hands than have met grief through flying accidents. Someone sawing right through a mainspar in order to move a machine in a hurry (and this has happened) causes irretrievable terminal damage, but with a properly controlled and responsible flying operation an incident such as an occasional forced landing normally results in a readily repairable situation, if any damage at all.

Aeroplanes were built to fly; that is why they were given wings. Only by seeing a machine in action can a person fully appreciate the achievements, the limitations, the rate of progress and the other factors that have enabled aviation to reach its present levels within the span of one human lifetime — and *only* at the Shuttleworth Collection at Old Warden in Bedfordshire can it all be seen still today.

Above: Included among several foreign aircraft in the Strathallan Collection is a Fokker S11 Instructor side-by-side basic trainer. The type first appeared in 1947 and was built in Italy as the Macchi M416 and under licence in Brazil. PH-ANK served with both the Dutch Air Force and the Dutch Navy before arrival at Strathallan in 1977.

All pictures in this feature were supplied by R. E. Richardson, Manager, Strathallan Aircraft Collection.

Strathallan Aircraft
Collection

TWO FEATURES of the Strathallan Aircraft Collection make it unique. The first is that it has been created by one man and the second is that it almost happened by accident!

Sir William Roberts had only wanted to acquire the Hawker Hurricane, G-AWLW, when it was advertised for sale in late 1969 but its owner was only prepared to sell it as part of a 'package' including two Spitfire T9s. The aircraft were eventually purchased and flown to Shoreham in April 1970. One of the Spitfires was restored and flown while the Hurricane was stripped down for a total rebuild which included the removal of a number of 'unusual' modifications incorporated during its first rebuild in Canada some years before. The second Spitfire, G-AWGB, was sold to Canada where it was re-converted to a single-seater and flown as CF-RAF.

The following year it was decided to move the aircraft to Strathallan, a small grass airfield near Auchterarder and which was on Sir William's Scottish estate. An AT-6 and a Harvard had been added by then and two dismantled Tiger Moths were already in residence at Strathallan. By now Sir William had made up his mind to create the most comprehensive collection of *flyable* World War II machines that would be possible. He concentrated on those types which had been flown by the RAF. Few machines were available in the UK and therefore he scoured the world — particularly Australia and Canada, in order

Above: General view of the fine new Museum at Strathallan.

Top right: Strathallan's oldest flying aircraft, the 1934 DH85 Leopard Moth G-AIYS, started its working life in Egypt, was acquired in 1946 by Mr Ted Gardner and restored by him, to win the John Randall Trophy for best vintage aircraft in 1976; it arrived at Strathallan in April 1977.

Centre right, above: After a first flight in March 1946, the Percival P40 Prentice was adopted as a standard basic trainer by the RAF. Strathallan's example, G-AOLU, served with the RAF from 1948 to 1956 and is preserved in its service identity as VS356.

Centre right, below: The Miles M17 Monarch was a three-seat cabin successor to the Magister trainer and first flew in 1938. Most of the few built served with the RAF during WW2 but Strathallan's G-AFLW was owned by Rolls-Royce Ltd at Hucknall for nearly 20 years.

Bottom right: Most famous of *ab initio* trainers and most numerous preserved aircraft in flying condition is the Tiger Moth. This one, DH82A, was built by Morris Motors in 1942 and joined Strathallan in 1967 after service with the RAF and, from 1953, with Orkney Flying Club as G-ANFV.

to fill gaps in the collection. As a result the visitor to Strathallan can now view a Lockheed Hudson, Westland Lysander, Bristol Bolingbroke, Fairey Battle, DH Mosquito and Avro Lancaster in addition to the original Hurricane and a wide variety of second-line machines.

The collection has managed to add examples of civil types too including the Puss Moth, Hornet Moth, Leopard Moth, Dragon and Dragon Rapide from the DH stable and some more-exotic types such as the GAL Cygnet, BA Swallow and Miles Monarch.

In its first few years many of the exhibits were stored, crated or undergoing restoration but the limited hangarage has now been greatly expanded and, under the supervision of manager Dick Richardson, the visitor is now able to view not only the fully restored and airworthy machines but also many of those which are still actually undergoing restoration.

Above: Strathallan's GAL42 Cygnet II, the first British all-metal tricycle-undercarriage aeroplane and the only known surviving Cygnet. It was built in 1941 and was impressed into RAF service where because of its tricycle gear — a rarity then — it was used to familiarise Boston aircrew trainees.

Centre left: One of about eight de Havilland aircraft in the Strathallan Collection, the DH94 Moth Minor G-AFPN represents the last of the famous Moth line and differs from other Moths in being built entirely of wood and having a cantilever wing. It was built in 1939 and served in RAF Training Command throughout WW2.

Bottom left: Last of the RAF's piston-engined basic trainers was the Hunting Percival Provost, and it had only a brief service career before being superseded by the Jet Provost. WV493 was built in 1953 and served with 6 FTS and the Halton Apprentice TU before acquisition by Strathallan in 1975.

Above: Canadian-built is SAC's North American Harvard IIb advanced trainer G-AZBN. It was acquired from Holland in 1971 and refurbished as FT391, from the block of serials allocated to Harvards for the RAF and Commonwealth.

Centre left: SAC's Reid & Sigrist Desford VZ728, here seen with the Strathallan Hurricane flying overhead, is quite unique. It was built in 1945 as a twin-engined initial trainer but was later given an elongated nose for prone-pilot test flying.

Bottom left: Strathallan's representative of the famous Hawker Hurricane is a Mark IIb 12-gun machine built in Canada in 1942 with a Packard Merlin engine and Hamilton propeller. After retirement from RCAF service it was brought to Britain for the *Battle of Britain* film and then bought by the Collection and completely refurbished with R-R Merlin/Dowty power plant and given the markings of 605 Sqn RAF and the late Sqn Ldr Archie McKellar DSO DFC. It is the only civilian Hurricane flying, serialled G-AWLW.

45

Right: Strathallan's representative of the remarkable DH98 Mosquito is B35 G-ASKB, one of the last to be built in 1946. It served with the RAF before passing to a film company in 1962 to feature in *Mosquito Squadron* and *633 Squadron*, and then to the Collection in 1971. Here it is seen at West Malling in 1975 burning off inhibiting oil as the engines are started after seven years at rest.

Above: The Lockheed Hudson was the RAF's first WW2 American aeroplane; it was also the first RAF machine to shoot down a German — a Do18 on 8 October 1939, the first US-built machine to be ferried by air over the Atlantic, and the first RAF machine to sink a U-boat by rocket. Strathallan's Hudson IV G-BEOX saw action with the R Aus AF in 1942 and was flown from Australia in 1973 to be painted in its original wartime markings of 13 Sqn RAAF.

Right: The flying of veteran aeroplanes demands much work behind the scenes. Here in Strathallan's engineering hangar is Hurricane G-AWLW being prepared for flight.

The policy of Sir William Roberts for the Strathallan Collection is to restore to flying condition as many as possible of its aeroplanes. As many restorations are necessarily very lengthy, each aircraft or major component of an aircraft as acquired is brought and maintained to a state in which it is an exhibit in its own right while awaiting or undergoing full restoration. Three aircraft in this category are *(above)* Canadian-built (Bolingbroke) Bristol Blenheim IVT 9940, *(left)* Westland Lysander III G-AZWT and *(below left)* Fairey Battle I R3950.

Weekend in the Country

Neil Williams

This article first appeared in Shell Aviation News *No 442/1977 and is reproduced here by kind permission of that journal's editor. Since it was written, the author has been killed in a flying accident while ferrying a Spanish-built version of the Heinkel He111 from Spain to England. Well-known for his international success in the aerobatic field, Neil Williams also had a specific interest in older and more obscure aeroplanes, which called for a very different approach and a different scale of handling techniques. He excelled in both spheres. Neil was a total flying person and this report is published as a form of memorial to him, to his determined enthusiasm for improving the art and for his special natural abilities as a pilot.*

DURING MAY 1977 the Queen's Silver Jubilee Air Pageant was held at White Waltham, in Berkshire. I had been asked by the Shuttleworth Collection to demonstrate its 1912 Blackburn Monoplane at this two-day event; the Rothmans Aerobatic Team, too, wanted me to take my old Number 4 position for its last displays before final disbandment. I had been in at the beginning of the team, when in 1970 the late Manx Kelly formed it with Stampe biplanes. Now I was to be in at the finish, but this time flying the high-performance Pitts S2A.

With only two items each day I began to look forward to a quiet weekend at a pleasant grass airfield in the country. Certainly it would be a holiday compared to a normal summertime weekend. I might actually be able to watch most of the display, something I am rarely able to do. There would have to be an early morning's air test on the Blackburn, which was to be transported to White Waltham by road and assembled for the show; since rotary engine time is measured in minutes rather than hours this meant just a quick circuit to prove all systems. True, there was still some administrative work to look after, as I had arranged for a Spitfire IX to take part in the Biggin Hill Air Fair — held at the same time as the Jubilee Pageant — but all I had to do was brief the pilot when he arrived from overseas. I should have known that things were going too well. At the last moment he sent a message to say he couldn't come! I studied the programmes for the pageant and the Air Fair. If I based the Spitfire at White Waltham, could I fly over to Biggin, display the aircraft and return in time for

Left: Neil Williams, as best remembered by the thousands to whom he gave so much pleasure. / *Mike Jerram*

Above right: Neil Williams taking off in the Hon P Lindsay's Morane MS230. / *Mike Jerram*

Right: DH Mosquito B35 which Neil Williams flew in the film *Mosquito Squadron*, pictured at Booker in September 1971 just before it left for the Confederate Air Force base in the US. / *Stuart Howe*

my other commitments? I decided that it was possible, but only if the Biggin Hill organiser agreed to bring my slot time forward. I rang him up . . . Yes, he said, that would be OK. By now it was beginning to turn into a standard flying-season weekend, though with careful planning there shouldn't be any rush between appearances. One big advantage of displaying high-performance machines is that one can cover a lot of ground quickly and thus take part in airshows a considerable distance apart. However, this does call for really accurate navigation — usually in an aircraft with no aids — and getting off track can ruin the afternoon for a lot of people. Even a slippage of a couple of minutes can make it impossible to reach the next site in time.

White Waltham also had a Spitfire on its programme, a Mark I flown by a colleague. With two Spitfires to be positioned from their home bases to White Waltham, we naturally decided to go in formation, for such an opportunity arises all too rarely.

The first day of the Jubilee Air Pageant dawned fair and clear. Crouched in my small cockpit I could scarcely tear my eyes away from the trim beautiful lines of the Mark I, as it gently rose and fell just beyond my wingtip. I pressed the R/T button: 'Spitfires, turning port — go!' and the horizon slanted as we swung on to the heading for White Waltham. For those who came early to the display, the sight and sounds that greeted them must have made it worthwhile as we broke into the circuit and landed, the Rolls-Royce Merlins crackling and popping as they were throttled back.

But now there was business to attend to, for as we taxied in I could see the Blackburn Monoplane being prepared for flight. We had decided to air test this early, before the daytime turbulence built up and the circuit became congested with visiting aeroplanes. From 1750hp to 50hp, I thought, as I used the brawny back of our engineer to climb into the cockpit.

The Gnome rotary burst into life on the first swing, but I had difficulty in establishing the correct positions of the control levers to achieve full power. There are three of these levers; an air slide, a petrol needle valve, and a throttle, the throttle being used only when the engine is running properly and the mixture has been set using the other two. One cannot simply open everything wide on a rotary or the whole thing will

flood and stop. Eventually I persuaded the engine to give its revs, but for some reason the levers were not in their accustomed places on the quadrant.

At last I was ready. Chocks were removed and willing hands clung to the tail while I stabilised at full power. I raised and lowered my arm, and with a strong push from the mechanics the Blackburn rolled across the grass and drifted into the air. I leaned off the petrol slightly to compensate for the richness due to centrifugal force with rising rpm, noting that she was slightly right wing heavy, but nothing to worry about. The engine note still did not sound right — I adjusted the levers to try and improve things.

I had just reached the end of the airfield at about 300ft, when the engine died! With no ASI or altimeter in this 65-year-old original one has to rely on feel and instinct. The ground ahead was no good, but the wind was light, so I started to turn. I could not get back on to the duty runway and there were tents and barriers across the airfield. Gliding silently downwards I pulled the petrol lever fully closed: if it had been a rich cut, this would cure it. At about 100ft I opened up . . . the Gnome coughed and restarted. It still wasn't right, but it gave enough power to climb, so I continued my circuit and landed on the runway. Evidently some new sparking plugs had been the problem. They were immediately removed and replaced by the older type which we knew to be satisfactory.

By this time the crowds were pouring in. We pilots assembled for our display briefing, during which I confirmed with Biggin Hill my arrival and departure slots in their Air Fair programme. There was time to get a bite to eat and a cup of tea, and then I had to prepare the Spitfire IX. It appeared that the ground crew were also away to lunch, so there was no starter trolley available. Not to worry, I still had an ace up my sleeve in the shape of two batteries in the rear fuselage instead of the usual one.

Again the airfield echoed to the well-known crackle, and soon the machine was bounding across the grass. In the cockpit the thunder of the Merlin was muted as I held hard right rudder to keep her straight against the enormous turning effect of the engine and propeller. The ground fell away, I quickly changed hands on the stick to select gear up, and pulled the power back to cruise as I turned on course for Biggin Hill. I trimmed out and changed frequency to London Radar; I would need a special VFR clearance, about which I had briefed Air Traffic. Everything was going like clockwork — London knew my details and confirmed radar identification, the weather was near perfect.

And then, almost imperceptibly, the note of the Merlin changed. It was so subtle that one could have been forgiven for missing it, but I knew this Spitfire well. I checked the engine instruments and saw the oil pressure was dropping!

Above left: Neil again, at the controls of the Shuttleworth Granger Archaeopterix. / *Air Portraits*

Left: Neil was seemingly at home in any and every flying machine, as here in the Shuttleworth reproduction of a 1910 Boxkite. / *Stuart Howe*

There was not a second to lose. I was flying a precious and historic aeroplane: one mistake could be catastrophic. I turned back and told London I was experiencing difficulties. I asked them to alert Biggin and Wycombe Air Park, where the aircraft was based; already I was thinking of how I could get to a suitable repair base. The oil temperature was rising, so I reduced power to the minimum and opened the radiator shutters to increase airflow through the oil cooler under the port wing.

White Waltham was now on the nose, but beyond, no more than ten miles away, was base. The pressure had stabilised at a low but safe reading though the temperature continued to rise slowly. I asked London to get through to Wycombe on the land line and find out the wind and runway in use. Clearing the zone I changed frequency, called the tower, pulled back the power, dropped the undercarriage and glided in to the grass runway, cutting the switches as I touched down. It was another week before we found the cause, a broken oil cooler bypass valve, but the engine had been shut down in time to save it.

With that emergency out of the way, I could now start thinking about displays again. How could I get back to White Waltham? I looked around the hangar and found a CAP 10 belonging to one of the aerobatic organisations, which I flew from time to time. Well, this was going to be one of those times! Then I had another thought. What if I could borrow the Spitfire I? I studied my watch: my Biggin Hill display was only forty minutes away — it couldn't be done. But supposing I tried for a later slot time?

Taking a chance on being able to use the Mk I, I telephoned Biggin, asking at the same time if they would accept a change of aircraft. They were surprised, but agreed. So, borrowing a headset, I leapt into the CAP 10 and was soon retracing my path towards White Waltham. I called the tower and asked them to broadcast for the Spitfire pilot to meet me when I landed. He too was a bit surprised, but agreed to my using the aeroplane after his own display was over. As he took off I was busy rushing about finding a fuelling truck, starter trolley and mechanics to turn the aircraft round. Even by Battle of Britain standards it was a record! From the Spitfire's touchdown to my getting airborne in it with a full tank of fuel was just five minutes.

London Radar was as helpful as ever, and I reached Biggin with two minutes to spare. The display itself was relaxing by comparison with what had gone before. Soon I was cruising westward again across the zone, leaving behind a commentator whose notes referred to a Spitfire IX and was later heard muttering 'I could have *sworn* it was an earlier mark' . . .

Back on the ground at White Waltham I was just in time for the Rothmans aerobatic team briefing. We had flown this routine many times during our recent two-month tour in the Middle East, and my only concern was that there might be a temptation to try that little bit too hard — the team had never had an accident in formation. Had I but known it, everyone else was thinking the same thing. The show was tight, clean, and above all safe. As our four Pitts S2As split in the final bomb burst, I thought 'We shall only be doing this once more'. Then we were down and taxying in, waving back to the crowd.

Walking down the line of aircraft towards the Blackburn, I saw that we had picked our time well. The wind had dropped and conditions were almost perfect. Seated precariously in the canoe-like fuselage, I scarcely dared breathe until we had reached a safe height from which I could make a glide landing. But the change of spark plugs had restored the engine performance, and I could confidently achieve full rpm. With the rev counter the one and only instrument in the aeroplane, it was reasonable to ask that it should present a decent reading! This time she was going so well that I had to throttle back to lose height, a most unusual situation.

So ended the Saturday display. But as I got into the CAP 10 to take it back to Wycombe, I found myself with a few more things to think about. It appeared that my colleague with the Spitfire Mk I, who had also been demonstrating a ferociously camouflaged Fiat G46 fighter trainer of the same vintage, was going motor racing the next day and had left both his aeroplanes for me to fly on the second day of the Air Pageant. My one experience of the Fiat dated from several years previously, when I had collided with a seagull which removed the leading edge of the wing all the way back to the main spar; that flight had been confined to a wide circuit and a fast straight approach to a wheel landing. Sunday was further complicated by a commitment I had made after the airshow to move a Spitfire Vc belonging to the Shuttleworth Collection from Duxford to Old Warden. Some assistance was clearly in order, so I co-opted my wife to do some ferry flying in our Jodel light aircraft.

The Spitfire Mk I having been returned to its base overnight, our first job on Sunday morning was to get over to Wycombe to collect it. Fortunately the weather remained fair, and after seeing my wife safely airborne again, I climbed into the Spitfire and pressed the starter button. Day Two had begun.

At White Waltham I taxied in and parked alongside the Fiat G46. Rather unwillingly I strapped into the front cockpit of this strange-looking machine, running

Right: The Belgian Stampe aerobatic biplane flown by Neil Williams as one of the Rothmans team before the change to the Pitts S2As. / *Mike Jerram*

Left: One of the Rothmans Pitts Specials in which Neil Williams demonstrated his extraordinary flying skill in many parts of the world.   *Stuart Howe*

Below: Neil Williams talking to ground crew after landing at Old Warden with Shuttleworth's Spitfire Vc from Duxford in May 1975. / *Air Portraits*

Right: Neil Williams on a test flight with the Warbirds of Great Britain's CASA 2.111 (Heinkel He111) from Blackbushe in November 1977. Neil and his crew, including his wife, died when a similar machine they were ferrying from Spain crashed on a mountain. / *Air Portraits*

over the briefing I had been given and identifying the unusual layout. I had been specially warned not to touch a cable that ran along the floor, whose function was to disconnect the front cockpit controls... Apparently this was to allow the instructor in the rear seat to save the day if the student panicked!

The engine, with its six stub exhausts, seemed to make up in noise for what it lacked in thrust, though the aeroplane went quite well on only 215hp. After fifteen minues, during which I managed to avoid any seagulls, I decided that I wouldn't attempt anything clever but merely fly low and make a lot of noise, keeping the manoeuvres to basic figures like loops, Cuban 8s and barrel rolls.

Then it was time for pilot briefing. My flying programme was now so full that I gave my lunch ticket to one of the Shuttleworth team in exchange for a home-packed sandwich, and started up the still-warm Fiat for the first display of the day. The technique of 'low and noisy' seemed to go down well, and it also allowed me to assess the wind before my Spitfire I event.

For me, flying a Spitfire is a never-ending delight. All too soon my display was over, but I could look forward to a second run as I set course for Biggin Hill once more. Biggin sounded surprised to hear me, for I had been unable to telephone them before take-off and was adhering to my programmed time. What I didn't know was that they had misunderstood the previous day's message and therefore assumed I wasn't coming on the Sunday. 'You're cleared to land', they said. 'We can fit you in at 17.00 hours.'

'Negative', I called, mindful of my fuel state and the fact that I had a two-minute gap allotted for my landing back at White Waltham.

ATC then queried: 'Can you display at 15.15?'

'Negative, my landing slot is 15.06 at Waltham.'

'Stand by', replied ATC . . . then after a pause, 'How about 14.35?'

'Affirmative', I said, clinching the deal. A camouflaged shape rocketed up past me, waggling its wings: it was the Royal Naval Sea Fury, at the end of his show, bound for the Air Pageant at Waltham. I rocked my wings in reply, opened the radiator shutter and eased the rpm up to 2650 as I lowered the nose. My watch showed 14.35. Nine minutes later I completed a climbing roll and levelled out on course for the west.

In the shallow orbit over White Waltham I watched the Sea Fury display, then it was my turn to join the circuit and land. More out of habit than the expectation of finding anything wrong, I walked around my aeroplane, and was horrified to discover a large dent in the bottom cowling with blood and feathers everywhere. A bird had gone clean through the propeller, missing both the oil tank and the carburetter intake by inches. And the owner of the Spitfire was also the owner of the Fiat!

Happily there was no real damage — only a panel that could easily be straightened. I put it out of my mind as I climbed into the Pitts, for now I had to concentrate and fly steadily. For the final bow-out of the Rothmans Aerobatic Team we all wanted a safe polished performance.

Despite my inner misgivings the team acquitted themselves with honour. 'This really is the last time' I reflected, as we burst downwards and I cut the smoke in the pullout. Perhaps the old Blackburn was getting jealous of the way I was consorting with these modern machines; at any rate, I had just stabilised on the chocks at full power when there was a loud 'twing' and everything went quiet. The large crowd, primed by the commentator, waited, hushed and expectant. No problem, three of the ignition wires had come adrift and tied themselves in a knot: this could soon be sorted out. We reconnected the wires, but still the Gnome showed no signs of life, whereupon it was discovered that the carbon brush had fallen out. After a futile ten minutes on our hands and knees in the oil-soaked grass under the aeroplane we were forced to call it a day.

All that now remained was to set course in the Jodel for Duxford, and the Spitfire Vc. Even after two consecutive days of Spitfire displays I could not resist a loop and a couple of rolls en route to Old Warden, especially as the clipped wings of the Mk Vc positively demanded that they be rolled! We pushed her into the hangar and took off for the last leg of the weekend, making it with 30 seconds to spare before Wycombe airfield closed.

It was wonderful to relax at last in the hotel, where the rest of the Rothmans group were assembling for the team's farewell party. A few minutes later one of the executives arrived, looking a little flustered. 'The traffic', he explained apologetically. 'You've no idea . . . '

Fleet Air Arm Historic Flight

Below: The first of more than 1700 Fairey Firefly fighter/recce aircraft built for the Royal Navy entered service in 1943 and consequently the type saw considerable active service, but Firefly WB271 is a Mk 5 machine that started with 814 Sqn in 1949. It saw service in the Korean war and then with the Royal Australian Navy until scheduled for scrapping in 1966. Officers of HMS *Victorious*, then visiting Sydney with 814 Sqn embarked, saved it from that fate and brought it home for presentation to the Fleet Air Arm Museum and renovation. WB271 is appropriately finished in the colours it wore while in Korea with 814 Sqn.

FROM A very modest beginning with three aircraft in 1963, the Fleet Air Arm Museum at Royal Naval Air Station Yeovilton has expanded greatly in every particular — in total area and covered space, in the number and significance of exhibits, in importance as a source of authentic information on all aspects of naval aircraft and in the number of visitors. The Museum is established as an independent educational Trust and the level of sustained interest is such as to justify year-round opening, except for two weeks covering Christmas and the New Year.

Apart from the airworthy machines of the Historic Flight, there are about 40 static aircraft on display at Yeovilton and more are held in reserve, bringing the total of aircraft owned to 56. In addition there are numerous models and other lesser exhibits, all labelled and backed up with informative literature available from the shop and books in the library, and generally displayed in logical order to illustrate the part played by naval aviation since the early years of this century.

On exhibition in the outside display area of Yeovilton, where most of the post-World War II FAA aircraft are to be seen, is Concorde 002, which has nothing to do with naval flying but attracts considerable interest. The machine is the first British-built Concorde; it is owned by the Science Museum and, when its long period of proving and development

Left: Line-up of Fleet Air Arm Historic Aircraft Flight, with visitors, at the Royal Naval Air Station, Yeovilton (HMS Heron) Somerset. / *HMS Heron*

Preparing the Flight's Sea Fury for flight; *(bottom left)* the pilot signing the form 700, *(right)* taxying to start of take-off run, and *(below)* spreading the wings. / *all HMS Heron, LA(Phot) T. J. Tierney*

Above: The Flight's Sea Fury FB11 TF956 was the first of 565 built by Hawker Aircraft from 1948. It saw service with 802 NAS and on various air stations before a period in Korea with 807 NAS from HMS *Theseus*, where it flew about 200 operational sorties. After further service with various units and a period with Airwork on Fleet Requirement duties, TF956 was bought back by the Hawker Company for resale abroad; instead it was selected for renovation to join the Hawker historic collection but pressure of work caused the company to offer it to the Royal Navy in 1970 provided the restoration was completed. / *Mike Jerram*

flying was completed, it was offered for display at Yeovilton to give the public an opportunity of seeing it at close quarters.

The machines of the Historic Flight itself are not part of the exhibition, but they can sometimes be seen in the air by visitors to Yeovilton. Like all historic aircraft maintained in flying condition, they work to a full and very exacting programme of engagements during the display flying season. It is intended to add another notable FAA aircraft to the active list of machines shown in the pictures. One of the present static exhibits, a Seafire 17 built in 1948, is to be restored to flying condition and, one hopes, will be seen performing with the venerable Swordfish, Sea Fury and Firefly before too long.

Right: Wren mechanics of HMS Heron turning the engine of Sea Fury the hard way during routine maintenance.
HMS Heron, T. J. Tierney

Below: The Fairey Swordfish TSR2 'Stringbag' is legendary and LS326, as the one flying aircraft of three preserved Swordfish, is a worthy memorial to a worthy aeroplane. LS326 is a Mk 2 machine built by Blackburn Aircraft in 1943; it never saw active service but was one of the display of Victory aircraft in Hyde Park in 1945. It was then bought by Fairey Aviation Company and stripped and rebuilt 10 years later to be finished in original colours and lettered 5A to represent the leading aircraft from HMS *Ark Royal* in the *Bismarck* attack, for the film *Sink the Bismarck*. Westland Aircraft, having absorbed Fairey Aviation, in 1960 presented LS326 to the Royal Navy and Yeovilton has maintained it in flying condition ever since.

Where Historic Aircraft Fly

Gordon Riley

THE SMALL NUMBER of collections of flyable historic aeroplanes is a reflection of the costs and complexities which are involved in their acquisition, restoration and subsequent upkeep. This is particularly obvious when compared with the relatively large number of collections of veteran and vintage motor vehicles which exist and which are frequently maintained by a single owner.

Although there are many collections of preserved aeroplanes throughout the UK only three can claim to maintain their exhibits in airworthy condition. The Shuttleworth Collection, which dates back to R. O. Shuttleworth's private collection of the 1930s, the Duxford Collection and the Strathallan Aircraft Collection. The last two have been established since 1970 as a result of the fairly recent upsurge in interest in old aircraft. In addition to these three, mention

should be made of the Leisure Sport collection at Thorpe Water Park, Surrey, which provides a very interesting selection of types.

The majority of those historic aeroplanes which remain in airworthy condition are owned by individuals rather than by collections. Mainly as a result of operating costs they tend to be restricted to those types which were originally intended for private owners. Few collectors can afford to support an airworthy combat type although they are by no means unknown.

Whereas owning a historic motor vehicle would be within the reach of many individuals the possibility of owning an aeroplane of similar vintage is rather further removed. Not only must problems of maintenance, hangarage, insurance and spares be overcome, one must also consider the costs of learning to fly, the handling problems associated with older types and the simple fact that few aeroplanes are built in the numbers associated with motor vehicles and therefore they are correspondingly more difficult to discover. Indeed it could be fairly safely assumed that there are probably no more vintage aeroplanes left to discover in the UK — although we can always live in hope!

Below: The late Ormond Haydon-Baillie, one of Duxford's pioneer private owners, in his Canadair Silver Star G-OAHB. His collection is now maintained by his brother Wensley. / *Gordon Riley*

THE MAJOR COLLECTIONS
Duxford

The growth of Duxford as one of the major European centres of aircraft preservation and restoration is almost entirely due to the inspired partnership of a national museum — the Imperial War Museum — and a group of willing enthusiasts — initially the East Anglian Aviation Society and latterly the Duxford Aviation Society.

Duxford was declared surplus to requirements by the Ministry of Defence in 1968 and three years later, after abortive plans for its use as either a sports centre or a prison site, the Imperial War Museum was given permission to utilise one of the empty hangars as storage for its embryo aircraft collection. During the next two years the number of aircraft grew to ten, some purely stored and others undergoing restoration to display standard.

By 1973, when all other plans for the site's development had been abandoned, the museum decided to use Duxford as its main storage centre and in October that year an air display was mounted. This was in co-operation with the East Anglian Aviation Society and was sponsored by Ciba-Geigy (UK) Ltd. This display was the first opportunity for the public to view the nucleus of the Reserve Collection. A limited display was held in June 1974, followed by an ambitious two-day flying display in June 1975 which drew capacity crowds despite the inclement weather. The result of this public support was that the Museum was able to open Duxford on a daily basis after the 1976 Air Day.

Much of the day-to-day running of the Collection and virtually all of the restoration work is carried out by members of the Duxford Aviation Society. Formed in 1975, the Society has been enrolled as a Corporate Friend of the IWM and in the short time that it has

Below: Ormond Haydon-Baillie's Hawker Sea Fury FB11 G-AGHB/WH589. / *Duxford Aviation Society*

been in existence it has built itself a formidable reputation.

Special teams of members, each led by an experienced aeronautical engineer, are created to work on particular projects within the Collection. These include the B-17 Fortress *La Duxford Belle*, the Shuttleworth Collection's Spitfire Vb, the IWM RE8 and a privately owned P-51D Mustang, to name just a few. The Society also has a collection of its own which includes several recently retired jet fighters such as the Saab Draken and a number of airliners which range from a DH Dove to Concorde 01!

One of the features of Duxford is that a large number of the types on show are on loan from private individuals. These may range from a single aircraft, such as the Fairchild Argus owned by Winston Ramsey, Editor of *After the Battle* magazine, to whole collections such as that of the late Ormond Haydon-Baillie. Although primarily concerned with aircraft of a military nature Duxford provides a home for a tremendous range of machines from the delicate wooden gliders of the Russavia Collection up to the jet-powered Lightning and Victor. The collection is probably the most interesting of any within the UK and the fact that many of the exhibits are airworthy is an added attraction which makes it a must for all lovers of old aeroplanes to visit.

Although the major flying event is the annual Air Day, normally held in June, the nature of the collection means that a visit on any fine weekend throughout the year may be rewarded with the sight of one of the privately owned machines being flown. If it is during the display season it is quite likely that the Fortress, Spitfire or Varsity could be leaving or returning from a display elsewhere. Additionally, the DAS is promoting the use of the field for rallies and club flying and once the new grass runways are operational it is quite likely that Duxford will emerge as one of the busiest centres of vintage flying in Europe.

Above left: The Boeing B17G Fortress G-BEDF, owned by Euroworld Ltd and based at Duxford. / *Duxford Aviation Society*

Left: The well-known Nord 1002 G-ATBG, owned by L. M. Walton is Duxford-based; here it is painted to represent a Messerschmitt Bf108. /*Jeff Ball*

Above: This recently acquired Grumman TBM Avenger is to be restored to flying condition by DAS members at Duxford. / *Clive Norman*

Old Warden

In the years before the outbreak of World War II there were one or two pioneer collectors of historic aeroplanes, one of whom was Richard Shuttleworth. Following his death, in a wartime flying accident with the RAF, his mother formed and endowed a trust in his memory to provide an educational centre for 'the teaching of the science and practice of aviation and of afforestation and agriculture . . . '

The work of the Shuttleworth Collection is fully explained elsewhere in this book. Suffice to say that it is Europe's only range of flying aeroplanes dating from 1909 onwards to World War II and beyond. Flying Days are held on the last Sunday of each month from Easter to October and Old Warden is frequently the venue for rallies and competitions on other weekends throughout the summer. Duxford is only 40 minutes drive away and a visit to both collections can be easily accomplished in one day.

Admission: Daily, 11am-5pm. For details of flying events when higher charges may apply contact the Imperial War Museum, Duxford Airfield, Duxford, Cambridge CB2 4QR (telephone Cambridge 833963). The airfield is approximately eight miles south of Cambridge on the A505 Royston-Newmarket road.

Admission: Daily. For details of Flying Days apply (stamped, addressed envelope) to The Shuttleworth Collection, The Aerodrome, Old Warden, Biggleswade, Bedfordshire (telephone Northill 288). The aerodrome is close to the A1 near Biggleswade and is well signposted.

Strathallan

The Strathallan Aircraft Collection is described and illustrated in Chapter 4. It holds at least one flying display every year, generally in July, and the airfield is also the base of a parachuting club. The aircraft are rarely seen south of the border but local flying displays such as the Prestwick Air Day and the Scottish Air Show will generally boast at least one of them as part of the programme. As the collection becomes more firmly established it may be possible to look forward to participation in air shows further afield.

Admission: Daily, April-October, 10am-5pm. Further details from Strathallan Aircraft Collection, Strathallan Airfield, Auchterarder, Perthshire PH3 1LA (telephone Auchterarder 2545).

Thorpe Water Park

The Leisure Sport Collection started with the acquisition of one or two ex-FAA machines which would complement the predominantly maritime exhibits at Thorpe. As the Sea Vixen, Sea Hawk and Whirlwind were being delivered work was proceeding on the construction of a full-scale flying replica of one of the most famous maritime aircraft of all time — the Supermarine S5. After initial handling problems were ironed out the S5 replica has now been seen at a number of UK air shows and is certainly a magnificent sight.

Leisure Sport is building up a collection of flyable and static replicas of World War I combat types at Thorpe. The Sopwith Camel and Fokker DrI Triplane were demonstrated during the 1977 display season, along with the 'circus' of three Tiger Moths and the Fairchild Argus hack. these are due to be joined by a second Camel, Clerget-powered this time, and examples of the Fokker DVII, Albatross DV and de Havilland DH2.

To provide background effect a number of non-flying replicas are also being assembled at Thorpe, one of which is the Vickers Viking amphibian flying-boat that was used in the film *The People that Time Forgot*. Whether Leisure Sport will be able to mount full-scale flying displays at Thorpe, which is under the approach

Below: The Leisure Sport Camel replica pictured here is powered by a Warner Super Scarab radial engine. A second replica, however, has a genuine Clerget rotary. / *Gordon Riley*

Above: Also Scarab-powered is the Leisure Sport Fokker DrI replica G-BEDR. / *Mike Jerram*

to Heathrow airport, will remain to be seen but judging by the company's participation in 1977 air displays at White Waltham, Booker and Blackbushe it is certain that its aircraft will not be far from the public eye.

Admission: For details contact Leisure Sport Ltd, Eastley End House, Coldharbour Lane, Thorpe, Egham, Surrey TW20 8TD (telephone Chertsey 64142).

AIRFIELDS FREQUENTLY USED BY VINTAGE AIRCRAFT

There are a number of airfields around the country which are hosts to vintage aircraft and at which a visitor might see interesting machines in the air. However, it cannot be stressed too strongly that these airfields are private property, as are the aircraft which they house and that casual visitors who arrive unannounced are generally not welcome, other than in public car parks or enclosures. Most of the companies mentioned are aware of the public interest in the aircraft which they own or maintain and will be happy to let visitors look at them if *prior permission* has been obtained in *writing*. Please remember, this section is merely intended as a *guide* and should under *no circumstances* be taken as an open invitation to wander around an active airfield.

Blackbushe Airport
near Camberley, Surrey

Plans for the establishment of an aircraft museum at Blackbushe were first announced some years ago but lack of planning permission has held up the construction work. Nevertheless the nucleus of a collection of flying aircraft has been set up and other interesting types are frequently to be seen passing through.

Warbirds of Great Britain Ltd, a company based at Blackbushe, has been responsible for the import and export of a number of ex-military types in recent years. Activity has been mainly concentrated on Hawker Sea Fury target-tugs from West Germany and ex-Spanish Air Force CASA 2.111 and CASA 352 (licence-built Heinkel He111 and Junkers Ju52/3m) machines. Besides these types the company has been involved with a Spitfire 16, Hispano HA1112M-1L (licence-built Messerschmitt Bf109), Sopwith Pup replica and Gloster Meteor TT20.

Above left: This CASA 352 is based at Blackbushe with the Warbirds of Great Britain collection. It has been used for film and TV work masquerading as a Junkers Ju52/3m. / *Paul Cordwell*

Left: The only remaining Sea Fury of a batch imported from West Germany is this example; now coded MW-S, it is owned by Mike Stow. / *Paul Cordwell*

Above: Spitfire IX MH434 is owned by Adrian Swire and based at Booker with Personal Plane Services Ltd. It is seen here at Duxford with the late Neil Williams in the cockpit. / *Jeff Ball*

Right: Also owned by Adrian Swire is Dragon Rapide G-AKIF. / *Paul Cordwell*

A flying display is usually held in August each year under the auspices of the Blackbushe Airport Users' Association and aircraft from the Warbirds collection are generally on show and may fly. Owing to the nature of the business it is difficult to say precisely what one is liable to see at the field but visitors can generally expect to see at least one or two machines parked next to the public car park. Please remember that this is a private airfield, visitors may obtain further information from Warbirds of Great Britain Ltd, Blackbushe Airport, near Camberley, Surrey.

Booker Airfield, (Wycombe Air Park), near Marlow, Bucks

The collection of historic aircraft and replicas which was built up and maintained by the late Doug Bianchi of Personal Plane Services Ltd is near-legendary. Although the company has always been associated with unusual aeroplanes, the first replica was the Vickers Type 22, built in the late 1950s, which was later used in the film *Those Magnificent Men in Their Flying Machines*. PPS Ltd handled all the technical side of the film and provided a pair of Santos Dumont Demoiselle replicas too.

After this involvement a Fokker EIII replica was built and flown together with a Pfalz DIII, the latter for use in the film *The Blue Max*. More recent

Above: A favourite with vintage owners and flyers is the Piper P3 Cub. G-ASPS is seen here at Booker. / *Mike Jerram*

additions include the Morane Type N and the Manning-Flanders MF1 replicas.

As well as its own aircraft the company restores and maintains a considerable number of privately owned machines including two Spitfires, two Dragon Rapides, two Yakovlev C11s, a Harvard, a Fiat G46 and the recently restored Westland Lysander of Phillip Mann. A Sopwith Triplane replica is currently under construction for the Hon Patrick Lindsay.

Wycombe Air Park is a busy aerodrome and Personal Plane Services is a busy company. Neither takes kindly to uninvited 'guests' wandering among the aeroplanes but the view from the public car park is usually graced by the sight of one or two of the historic aircraft parked on the apron. A flying display is usually held in September each year, in conjunction with a vintage vehicle rally, and this is recommended as the best time to visit the field to be certain of seeing some of the veterans in the air.

RAF Coningsby
Royal Air Force Battle of Britain Memorial Flight

RAF Coningsby, in Lincolnshire, is the home of one of the RAF's most unusual units, the Battle of Britain Memorial Flight. Familiar to millions all over the country and in Europe the Flight is a firm favourite with air show crowds and certainly provides an impressive sight with its Lancaster, flanked by a Spitfire and Hurricane. Chapter 1 covers it in detail.

The Flight has a total of seven aircraft on strength, two Spitfire PR19s, a Spitfire V, a Spitfire IIa, two Hurricanes and the Lancaster B1. A team of specialist engineers and pilots keep the aircraft in pristine flying trim and air time is strictly limited in order to preserve engine and airframe hours. Some years ago the Flight obtained four Rolls-Royce Merlins from an Argonaut airliner and with them it was estimated that the Hurricane could be kept flying for the next hundred years!

As Coningsby is an operational RAF base the public are not admitted to view the aircraft. If you are in the vicinity it is possible that a stop might be rewarded by the sight of some of the aircraft outside their hangar and if you are lucky one of them could be airborne on a test or pilot check flight.

Redhill Aerodrome
Surrey

In the lean years of the 1950s and early 1960s it was the Tiger Club of Redhill that provided a focal point for the art of aerobatic flying in the UK. This was achieved on a small number of special single-seat Tiger

Above: One of the stars of the Tiger Club fleet is the Arrow Active G-ABVE, which is now kept by Lewis Benjamin at Redhill and is seen here piloted by the late Neil Williams at Old Warden. */ Air Portraits*

Moths but as the Tiger became outclassed in competition aerobatics the club acquired a number of French and Belgian-built Stampe SV4s. Similar in appearance to the Tiger Moth, the Stampe has superior aerobatic qualities but is today considered to be totally outclassed in world-class aerobatics by more modern types such as the Pitts Special and the Yak 50.

The Tiger Club still provides many of the country's top aerobatic pilots and club machines are frequently used in competitions both at home and on the continent. Although one or two of the vintage types have been sold to private owners within the club the hangars at Redhill still have a good selection of interesting prewar types such as the Arrow Active and Percival Mew Gull, as well as many Stampes and Tigers and the circuit is generally graced with their presence most weekends.

It must again be stressed that there are *no* facilities at Redhill for the public to enter the airfield or hangars to view the aircraft at close quarters unless *written* permission has been obtained from the club before a visit. Enthusiasts do, however, have a chance to see

the club aircraft and pilots in action as they put on a small number of flying displays at various airfields throughout the summer months. These have included Rochester, Oxford and Booker in recent years.

RNAS Yeovilton
Fleet Air Arm Historic Aircraft Flight
As well as providing a home for the static aircraft of the FAA Museum, RNAS Yeovilton (HMS *Heron*) is the base for the aircraft of the Historic Aircraft Flight. Pictures appear in Chapter 6.

Originally composed of the solitary Fairey Swordfish LS326, this has now been joined by the Firefly AS5, two Sea Furies and a Tiger Moth. The Tiger came from the Royal Navy Gliding School but the others were from outside the Service. The Firefly was bought from an Australian scrapyard by the officers of HMS *Victorious*, the Sea Fury FB11 was presented by Hawker Siddeley Aviation Ltd and the two-seat Sea Fury came from West Germany where it had been used as a target-tug.

The aircraft of the Flight are not on view to the public at Yeovilton but are to be seen flying at most of the major air shows throughout the summer. If you are lucky a visit to the FAA Museum may be rewarded with the added bonus of one of the Flight machines in the air.

Owner's Organisations
With the high level of maintenance charges and lack of experience on vintage types now associated with many professional aircraft engineering companies there has

been a rise in the number of owners who now maintain their own aircraft. Until fairly recently most of this work was carried out under the supervision of the Popular Flying Association but the formation of the Vintage and Classic Aeroplane Association in early 1978 could lead to even more owners maintaining a wider variety of types than was possible under the earlier scheme. These various organisations cater mainly for their members needs and are therefore of a rather specialised nature but non-pilot members are always welcome, as are visitors to the rallies and fly-ins which are organised throughout the summer months at airfields up and down the country. Readers interested in visiting these events should contact the organisations direct or keep an eye on announcements in magazines such as *Flight International, Vintage Aircraft* and *Aircraft Illustrated.*

Popular Flying Association

The PFA is the governing body in the UK for all amateur-built and -maintained light aeroplanes. Although the PFA membership covers a wide range of types a good number of them are of the vintage variety and most of those aircraft which have been restored in recent years have been under PFA authority.

The Association holds an annual rally at Sywell aerodrome, near Northampton during the first weekend of July each year. This is the largest gathering of light aircraft in Europe, regularly attracting 400-500 aircraft per day to this small grass field. The visitors always include a good number of vintage types and Sywell is the premier rally of the UK calendar.

Although primarily intended for PFA members the public is encouraged to attend and there is always an interesting ground exhibition and an afternoon flying display. If you want to see some of the beautifully restored light aircraft now flown in this country come to Sywell and wait for them to come to you!

Further details from Popular Flying Association, Terminal Building, Shoreham Airport, Shoreham-by-Sea, Sussex.

Below: A big attraction at the 1977 PFA Sywell rally was the sole Spartan Arrow G-ABWP. It is owned by Raymond Blain and flew again after a 10-year rebuild by Roy Mills and associates. / *Gordon Riley*

Vintage Aircraft Club

Although it developed from the Vintage Aircraft Group of the PFA, the Vintage Aircraft Club can trace its ancestry back to the pioneer postwar enthusiasts who founded the Vintage Aeroplane Club at Denham in the early 1950s.

By the early 1960s it was clear to some pilots that many aircraft types were facing extinction and that something would have to be done if they were to fly anything other than the sophisticated American light aircraft which were then flooding the UK market. Many Proctors, Magisters and Messengers were scrapped simply because their wooden airframes made them awkward, and therefore expensive, to maintain. Types such as the Tiger Moth and Auster were luckier on account of their welded-tube fuselage structure but even they were facing the axe.

It was against such a background that a small group of enthusiasts met at Elstree aerodrome in 1964 with the aim of forming a group not just to preserve old aeroplanes but to *fly* them. The Vintage Aircraft Group changed its name to Club in 1973 and now boasts about 200 members owning 150 aircraft which range in size from an Aeronca 100 to a Spitfire.

The VAC is run by a committee of elected members who organise all of the activities. At least one weekend flying meeting is arranged every month — except December — and these are generally held on the first Sunday of the month at Finmere aerodrome, near Buckingham. During the summer the meetings can be more frequent and often take place at organised air shows where the members' aeroplanes are especially welcome on the programme.

Although many members are active pilots there is a large number who are not, many of them preferring to take photographs, swing a propeller or help to organise a spot-landing competition. It has long been club policy that all non-pilot members be encouraged to fly as passengers whenever space is available so if you are not content with admiring your favourite aeroplane from the 'wrong' side of the fence contact the Vintage Aircraft Club.

Further details from The Membership Secretary, Vintage Aircraft Club, 3 St Michaels Road, Sandhurst, Camberley, Surrey.

Below: Mike Stow brings his Bucker Jungmeister in to land at a Vintage Aircraft Club rally at Finmere, Bucks. / *Stuart Howe*

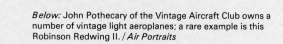

Below: John Pothecary of the Vintage Aircraft Club owns a number of vintage light aeroplanes; a rare example is this Robinson Redwing II. / *Air Portraits*

International Auster Pilot Club

The IAPC was founded in November 1973 with the intention of keeping Austers flying and, in doing so, to improve its image and make it into a desirable collector's item. The club's founder, Jim Sime, had seen many types dwindle until only a handful were left and he was determined that this fate should not befall the Auster — the only really successful postwar British light aeroplane. In the four years since its formation there has certainly been a very welcome upsurge in the Auster's popularity and several magnificent examples are now to be seen at club rallies.

Primarily in existence for the benefit of Auster owners and pilots the club has organised a preferential insurance scheme and a spares service — very useful when one considers that the Autocrat was withdrawn from production at the end of 1947. A measure of its success is the fact that membership is now in excess of 600 and is strong overseas as well as within the UK.

At least one club rally is held every year, in recent years these have been at Old Warden, and non-members are welcome to attend and view the selection of aeroplanes present. These can vary from the Taylorcraft Plus D (Auster Mk I) of 1939 up to the

Above: One of the most historic Austers still flying is Auster 5 G-AGOH, which acted as the engine test aircraft for the Cirrus Minor engine. It is preserved in flying condition by the Leicestershire Museum of Technology at Leicester East. */Iona Cruickshank*

final Austers built by Beagle Aircraft, the Airedale and Husky.

Membership is open to all interested in the history or operation of the Auster and further details are available from the Membership Secretary, Fennel House, Beryl Lane, Wells, Somerset.

de Havilland Moth Club

Although the Moth family of light aeroplanes is the most famous and prolific ever to have been produced in this country it was not until 1975 that an owner's club was founded to bring together pilots, restorers and enthusiasts of this legendary breed.

Stuart McKay's original intention was to start an organisation to help owners of Tiger Moths. The cost of commercially restoring one of these aircraft is

tremendous and therefore many owners were working towards rebuilding their own machines. A group which would co-ordinate their activities and arrange for the bulk purchase of materials and parts would obviously be of great help to all.

After inquiries from owners of other Moth types Stuart decided that the club should cater for all variants and membership has now been extended to cover all types of DH light aeroplane from the Humming Bird of 1923 to the Moth Minor — the last Moth of all.

The prototype Moth flew in February 1925 and during the following year it laid the foundations of the flying club movement as it is known today. During the next 14 years the de Havilland company built Moths in more numbers than any other British light aeroplane, before or since. The original Cirrus-powered DH60 was superseded by the immortal Gipsy Moth and this was finally developed into the Moth Major, the last example leaving the works in 1934. Other Moths which remain in existence include the Puss, Leopard, Hornet, Fox, Tiger and Moth Minor; the Giant Moth, Hawk Moth and Swallow Moth are sadly extinct. Member Tony Haig-Thomas is unique in that he owns an example of every type still existing, they are regularly flown and are one of the star attractions of the Historic Aircraft Museum at Southend Airport.

One or two rallies are held every summer but these are at different venues, further information and membership details are available from Stuart McKay, Tangmere, 16 Thatchers Drive, Maidenhead, Berks.

Vintage Glider Club

With the upsurge of 'high-technology' glass fibre and plastics sailplanes over the last ten years there had been a steady decline in the fortunes of the classic wooden gliders of the pre- and immediately postwar eras. The first International Vintage Glider Rally was held in 1973 and it was as a result of the interest shown at this rally that the Vintage Glider Club was founded.

Since 1973 there have been five more international rallies, held in Britain, Germany (Wasserkuppe), Switzerland (Gruyere), Britain again and Germany (Muenster). As well as these there have been countless local rallies at gliding sites throughout Britain in order to promote the sport of vintage glider flying.

Most of the vintage gliders in the UK are owned by individuals or small groups but there are two outstanding collections. Mike Russell's Duxford-based Russavia Collection boasts eight machines, of which the Slingsby Petrel is currently airworthy, while the Manuel Willow Wren is potentially the world's oldest flyable glider. At Tangmere Rodi Morgan has a small collection which includes the French Castel C25S, which flew as a prototype in 1942. He also has the 1935 Rhoensperber which won the 1939 British National Gliding Championships and which, when rebuilt, will be the last flyable example in the world.

Obviously the best place to see these beautiful old sailplanes is at one of the club rallies which are held throughout the summer at sites all over the country. For details of rallies and membership information contact the Hon Secretary, Otford House, Otford, near Sevenoaks, Kent.

The Vintage & Classic Aeroplane Association

The VCAA has been formed by representatives of various organisations connected with vintage flying — the DH Moth Club, the International Auster Pilot Club, the DHC1 Chipmunk Club and the Vintage Aircraft Club to name a few — to help promote interest, enthusiasm and participation in the sport and recreation of flying vintage and classic aeroplanes, and eventually to represent owners and operators of these aircraft, especially in matters of maintenance and airworthiness.

In Britain today there are over 600 'old' aeroplanes maintained in airworthy condition. Many are displayed during the summer months for the enjoyment of thousands of people. But, unlike modern training and business aircraft, most of these old machines are airborne for no more than one hour a week, and some for even less. People own and fly these aeroplanes for pleasure, not profit. When they were built they were constructed (very often by hand) by craftsmen who knew little of mass-production techniques and today's owner has soon to get acquainted with wood and fabric, glue and engine oil, in a way that 'new-generation' pilots will never have to experience.

Unfortunately, legislation has to move with the times; all the vintage and classic aeroplanes in the UK now represent only a small percentage of all the aircraft on the civil register but they are subject to the same varied and commercial pressures as their modern business and training counterparts. As a result, in recent years, many have been irreplaceably sold overseas, particularly to the United States.

The VCAA needs support from the general public if it is to help keep these aeroplanes where they belong. Members will be entitled to become directly involved in both the social and flying activities of the Association and will receive the quarterly magazine *Vintage Aircraft* as part of their membership. For further details and an application form write to The Membership Secretary, VCAA, Beryl House, Fennel Lane, Wells, Somerset. Membership categories: Family £10.00, Individual £7.50, Junior £5.00.

Below: This evocative shot of a Hornet Moth and a Tiger Moth seen through another Tiger's bracing wires sums up vintage flying. / *Stuart Howe*

Index